GREEK MYTHS

8 Short Plays for the Classroom

by

John Rearick

SCHOLASTIC
PROFESSIONAL BOOKS

New York • Toronto • London • Auckland • Sydney

DEDICATION

To Liz and the pirates in training.

Cover design by Vincent Ceci and Jaime Lucero
Cover Illustration by Lo Cole
Interior design by Carmen R. Sorvillo
Interior illustrations by David Diaz

ISBN 0-590-96383-X

Printed in the U.S.A.

TABLE OF CONTENTS

INTRODUCTION

As a teacher, I know that myths are a powerful classroom tool. Students who may be uninterested in language arts or history can be "grabbed" by these ancient stories. The student who didn't read anything before suddenly wants to read more myths—or "more of those stories about the gods and heroes," as he or she might say. Another student who's had trouble writing suddenly latches onto an assignment to write a myth. Often that one assignment branches into a series of activities or a group project. Students seem to know intuitively the importance of these tales.

Getting Started

What Is a Myth?

Scholars have spilled a great deal of ink trying to pin down just what the term "myth" means, but a neat definition has eluded them. The most manageable definition seems to be this: **A myth is a story, created collectively by a whole people or society over a period of time, that embodies some of the wisdom and truth valued by that society.**

In some cases, myths perform specific functions. Some, like the story of the first Narcissus flower, help explain why the natural world is the way it is. In other instances, myths seem to have been devised to answer deep philosophical issues. For instance, stories involving Cupid playfully explore the reason people fall in love with certain "targets," while other stories probe the reason evil exists in the world.

For many people, the word myth means simply a false story—and it is possible to read the Greek myths and dismiss each one. "There's no such thing as a Minotaur." "Sorry, no one can make wings out of wax and feathers and fly." "A Cyclops? Oh, come on!" But to dismiss the myths because of this would be to overlook the power of these stories and their ability to evoke feelings.

In discussions of the definition of "myth," I suggest that you follow your students' lead. Read one or two of the plays in class and then ask each student to come up with a definition for the word.

Who Wrote the Myths of Greece?

The Greek myths were created by a line of storytellers who added to and refined each other's work over the centuries. Their stories found their way into the literature that sprang

up when Greeks finally wrote down these oral traditions. You can find myths in the works of a variety of classical authors, including Homer, Hesiod, Sophocles, Euripides, Virgil and Ovid. It isn't uncommon for these authors to tell slightly different versions of the same myths—which is to be expected, given that they lived in a time frame that spans roughly 800 years.

The case of Homer illustrates just how difficult the question of authorship is. Some scholars believe that the historic event that served as the basis for the Trojan War stories took place around 1200 B.C. Those stories about the war probably circulated for about 400 years until they were pulled together and transformed into the two great epics we call the *Iliad* and *Odyssey*. Traditionally, those epics are said to have been composed—not actually written down—by a blind poet named Homer, who lived between 800 and 700 B.C. Yet very little is really known for sure about Homer. Many scholars believe that a poet named Homer really did live during that time—but was he really blind? Was he solely, largely or hardly responsible for the poems that were written down much later in his name? Indeed, did he have much if anything to do with the creation of the *Odyssey?* These and other questions remain mysteries. All that is known for certain is that the myths were created by Greeks long ago, and powerfully shaped that civilization's sense of itself and its place in the universe.

Who Are the Gods?

The figures that tower over these stories are the Greek gods. Before you begin reading these myths with your students you might want to spend some time discussing what the Greek gods are like. Here are some important points to highlight with your students.

- **The Greek gods did not always exist.** They themselves were created. According to the ancient Greek creation stories, heaven and earth existed before the gods. Then a race of supernatural beings, the Titans, came into being. The gods are in fact the grandchildren of the universe through the Titans.

- **Greek gods have human characteristics, including the weaknesses that mortals have.** In fact, it seems that the gods, with their prodigious powers, sometimes have even greater weaknesses than humans. They are not free from greed, envy, dishonesty or any of the common vices. In some cases, human heroes actually behave more nobly than the gods.

The Greeks and the Romans shared mythology, though they had different names for the same gods. With a few exceptions, this book uses the Greek names for the gods.

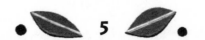

Why Teach Mythology?

The Greek myths have been taught for centuries. Recently, it seems, many teachers have been rediscovering the power that these stories have to enchant and inspire students. Here are some reasons you may want to use these tales in your classroom.

- **They are captivating reading.** Adventure, bravery, horror, love and fear are just a few of the issues that myths touch upon. In a way, these stories are the original high-interest readings. They have survived for centuries not because teachers have required them but because they have managed to keep people interested.

- **They are an important preparation.** As your students move into higher grades and start to read more literature, a knowledge of the Greek myths will be an important foundation. Having become acquainted with the stories of Daedalus, Odysseus and others, students will be able to understand references to these figures in works they will read later on.

- **They help teach writing.** Because myths contain powerful images and fantastic plots, they are very effective writing prompts. In this area, teachers can use myths in a variety of ways. Students can write their own myths in the style of the Greek stories. Alternatively, they can try to modernize one of the classical stories. They provide a great basis for teaching imaginative writing.

Why Use Classroom Plays?

Putting the Greek myths into a "readers' theater" format gives more students a chance to participate in a classroom activity. Instead of having students read paragraphs of a regular prose retelling of a myth, the readers' theater format allows students to read shorter, more accessible segments. For many students, the prospect of reading a few short lines at a time is far less intimidating than having to work through a block-like paragraph.

Playing dramatic roles also gives many students added classroom confidence, even as it builds their oral-presentation skills. Reading a character's role allows students to take on a playful identity for a short time. Students can have fun and enjoy presenting the story without having to worry about being judged for who they are.

These plays are designed for classroom use and therefore don't need any props or staging. But teachers who want to explore the dramatic possibilities of these plays may want to think about adapting these stories for a full stage production.

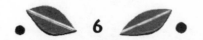

Using This Book

Every class is different, as is every student. As you adapt this material to best fit your own classroom, you might want to consider the following suggestions as you approach the plays.

- Consider reading the original myths before or after doing the play in order to put the material in context.

- Write the names of characters on the blackboard and review pronunciation before giving out the parts.

- Depending on the size of your class, you may want to assign two or three students to a part before you begin. In this way, students can switch into roles easily during a scene break. This will allow even more students to participate.

- At the end of each scene, take a break and ask a critical-thinking question. This will allow students to process what they've heard and clear some space for student questions.

- At the end of the reading, ask students to pick a character from the play and write a brief character study. Remind them to base their studies on specific events from the story.

- Ask the students if these stories have morals. Unlike Aesop's fables, these myths don't conclude with a succinct message. It's interesting to see what students make of these tales. Comparing the diverse interpretations will be an interesting classroom exercise.

- Each play in this volume is followed by a series of critical-thinking questions and some extension activities that you might want to use with your class. Review these items before you begin so that you'll feel comfortable with the material.

THE
PLAYS

THE GODS MUST BE CRAZY:

THE STORY OF CUPID AND PSYCHE

This story was written down by a Roman writer, but it's probably based on Greek sources. In this version we've used the Greek names for the gods, except one, Cupid. Most people know Cupid as the archer of love. In this myth a beautiful young woman named Psyche gets tangled up in a web of intrigue created by a jealous goddess, Aphrodite, and her son Cupid. Before the story ends Cupid's famous arrows will come into play, along with some nice ants, mean sheep with golden wool and a box that easily could be nicknamed "Pandora."

Characters (in order of appearance)

Zeus (ZOOS), the Greek's chief god; this play's narrator

Aphrodite (Af-ro-DI-tee), goddess of beauty

Sister 1

Sister 2

Psyche (SIGH-key), a beautiful human

Admirers (nonspeaking roles)

Cupid (KEW-pid), son of Aphrodite and god of love

Apollo, the god of the sun

Ant

Reed

Words to Watch For
Olympus (oh-LIM-pus), mountain home of the gods
Pegasus (PEG-uh-sus), horse with wings
Persephone (per-SEF-oh-nee), queen of the Underworld

Introduction

Zeus: Welcome to Mount Olympus! My name is Zeus and I'm going to be your host today. As top god here, I can assure you that we gods are very, very powerful—but we've also got our share of quirks. Some of us have been known to be silly, angry, or even downright jealous of you humans. . .

Aphrodite: Not me! No human could ever be as beautiful and popular as I am—and if anyone ever tried they'd be in big trouble.

Zeus: (to audience) See what I mean? Now today I want to tell you the story of a young woman named Psyche who had the sad luck to be born more beautiful—

Aphrodite: What?!

Zeus: —Sorry, I meant almost as beautiful as Aphrodite here. It's a story with lots of twists and turns, so stick close with me. . .

Scene One: Sisterly Love

Zeus: When Psyche was born, her parents couldn't believe what a cute baby she was. Later on, as she grew up, everyone admired Psyche's amazing beauty—everyone, that is, except her sisters.

Sister 1: What's she got that I haven't got? Why should so many men have crushes on her when clearly I'm more sophisticated and elegant?

Sister 2: And what about me? I don't deserve to be in the shadow of our little sister, either. What makes her think she's so great?

Zeus: But Psyche didn't have a swelled head from all the attention. When suitors came from all over Greece to ask her to marry them, she could hardly be bothered.

Psyche: (sighing as she spots two admirers following her. . .) Do these guys always have to follow me wherever I go? I can't even go down to the well without being followed by ten of them. I wish they'd go away.

Zeus: Aphrodite couldn't have agreed more with Psyche's wish. She knew the men following Psyche around had forgotten about her and her need for worship.

Aphrodite: If there's one thing I can't stand, it's a human who's competing with the gods. (shouting) Where's that son of mine?

Cupid: Right here, Mom. May I say that you look stunning today?

Aphrodite: Don't try to butter me up. I've got a job for you. Shoot one of your little magic arrows into Psyche and make her fall in love with a tree or a rock or—a skunk. That'll teach her a lesson.

Cupid: Anything you say, Mom. I'll be back in two shakes of Pegasus' tail.

Zeus: But when the winged archer flew to Psyche's home and got a better look at her, he had a change of heart.

Cupid: Wow, she's even prettier than—no, I'd better not say it. I can't make her fall in love with a skunk! I'll just put this arrow away and go home.

Zeus: As Cupid went to put the arrow away, though, he accidentally jabbed his finger with the arrow's tip. According to the magic arrow's rules, he was now sure to fall in love with the first person he saw. That person was the beautiful human, Psyche! It was his mother's worst nightmare, but he was never going to let her know. Instead, he set out to get help from his friend Apollo, the god of the sun—and fortune-telling.

Scene Two: Cupid's Scheme

Zeus: It wasn't long before Psyche's big stream of marriage proposals dried up, almost like magic, you might say.

Sister 1: Well, I guess there is some justice in the world.

Sister 2: We both married princes but our darling little sister hasn't landed anyone. Too bad. I'm all broken up about it.

Zeus: Psyche's parents feared that the gods now hated their youngest daughter for some reason, so they, too, went to the god Apollo for help.

Apollo: Your daughter's fate isn't a happy one. She's destined to be the bride of—well, a monster with wings who lives on top of a mountain. If you want the gods to be happy, you must leave her by the side of that mountain.

Zeus: It wasn't true. Cupid had told Apollo to say those things. But Psyche's parents didn't know that. With broken hearts they took her to the mountainside. As night fell, Psyche fought hard to keep up her guard. But the dark and cold were more than she could stand. A deep sleep fell over her. As she slept, a gentle wind magically picked her up and carried her to a hidden valley. When she woke up, she found herself on the steps of a huge golden mansion.

Psyche: Wh-where am I? (loudly) Hello? Anyone home? Could someone tell me whose house this is?

Cupid: (hiding behind a pillar) This is your house, Psyche, and I'm the husband the gods have chosen for you. (gushing) I love you, Psyche!

Psyche: (scared) You're the monster?

Cupid: (hurt) Well, actually I'm pretty okay-looking—and I'm not a monster!

Psyche: Then come out and let me see you.

Cupid: No. I want you to love me for who I am, not what I look like, or—or what my family is. I'll come visit you at night, when the house is dark. If you try to see me, all this will be ruined and we'll have to go our separate ways.

Zeus: We gods can be a little shy around humans. We prefer to be known from afar, which can be a problem if you happen to be married to a human.

Psyche: All right. . .Husband. I have to trust what you say.

Scene Three: The Light of the Lamp

Zeus: So the two lived quite happily in their new house. They talked all day, but Cupid didn't stop hiding himself from Psyche until night had darkened the house. Everything was going along amazingly well until Psyche began to miss her family.

Cupid: (from some hiding place) Are you happy, sweet Psyche?

Psyche: Yes, everything is quite lovely, but. . .

Cupid: But what? Let me know what's wrong and I promise I'll fix it.

Psyche: I want to see my sisters again. Could they visit me here?

Cupid: No. They'll ask too many questions.

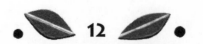

Psyche: But, you've already promised. Is your word meaningless?

Cupid: All right, they can come. But don't tell them anything about me!

Zeus: So it was arranged. Before long, the sisters were reunited.

Sister 1: Psyche, we thought you might be dead—but look at you, living in this house! That husband of yours must be one rich. . .monster! (giggles)

Sister 2: Tell all, Psyche! By the way, where is your husband? Does that monster mistreat you?

Psyche: He's not a monster! He's a—a young prince. (fibbing to cover what she doesn't know) He's away now visiting his father, the king, on important business.

Sister 1: Look at these jewels you have! What a collection!

Psyche: Oh, my husband's been collecting jewels for. . .for years. Right now he's. . .he's on an expedition to buy even more.

Sister 2: I thought you said that he was a young prince visiting his dad.

Psyche: (confused) Well, he is, sort of. . .Collecting jewels is his hobby, when he's not busy being a prince.

Zeus: Her sisters could tell that Psyche was making up stories. They insisted on the truth.

Psyche: (sadly) I don't know the truth, exactly. I know my husband is generous and kind, but I've never seen him.

Sister 1: You've never seen him?!

Sister 2: I wish I could say that about my husband.

Psyche: He won't show himself to me during the day. He says that we shouldn't worry about appearances.

Sister 1: Listen, sister, who's to say you're not married to a bloodthirsty monster? He could eat you alive at any moment! You've got to find out who he is!

Sister 2: Tonight, when he's asleep, sneak over to him with a lamp and get a good look.

Sister 1: But make sure you have a dagger in your hand. That way you can protect your-self if he tries to attack you!

Zeus: That night Psyche did as her older sisters suggested. She tiptoed over to her husband, got her dagger ready, then raised the lighted lamp over him.

Psyche: (whispering, in shock) It's Cupid! I'm married to the god of love!

Zeus: Her hands started shaking. The dagger fell from her trembling fingers, and a drop of hot lamp oil splashed onto Cupid's shoulder. That was some alarm clock!

Cupid: (sadly, rubbing his shoulder) So you didn't listen to me. Well, now that you've seen me. . .goodbye!

Psyche: No, wait, please!

Zeus: In a flash, Cupid and the house were gone. Psyche found herself sitting in an empty field, all alone. Realizing what she had lost, she began to cry.

Scene Four: Proving Her Love

Zeus: Psyche wasn't the sort of person to sit around and feel sorry for herself. She searched high and low for Cupid, and finally learned that he had gone back to live at his mother's house. Psyche dreaded having to speak with the great goddess of beauty, but in the end she went to the temple of Aphrodite to plead for Cupid's return.

Aphrodite: Well, look who it is. Don't you think you've caused enough trouble already?

Psyche: Please, goddess, tell me where I can find my husband.

Aphrodite: I've got him locked up safe and sound so he can recover from that nasty burn you gave him. You're not good enough to be my son's bride, anyway.

Psyche: Please don't talk to me like that!

Aphrodite: Are you willing to take a few tests to see if you deserve him?

Psyche: Yes, yes!

Aphrodite: Fine. Here's the first test!

Zeus: Aphrodite picked up three huge bags, each filled with a different kind of grain, and dumped them all out on the ground.

Aphrodite: Now pick up each piece of grain and put it back in the bag it came from, and have all the grains picked up by sundown. Got it? (laughs)

Psyche: Oh, no! I'll never be able to get that done. I'll never get Cupid back!

Zeus: Just then, a little ant heard Psyche's cry.

Ant: Come on, fellow ants, let's pitch in and help this poor creature.

Zeus: The ants swarmed over the pile of grain. Little by little, grain by grain, they filled up the sacks. By sunset, the job was finished, much to Psyche's joy and Aphrodite's disgust.

Aphrodite: (grunts) So, you did okay on the easy test.

Psyche: There's more?

Aphrodite: Of course! See way over there, those lovely gold-colored sheep? I want you to collect some of their pure-gold wool and bring it back to me. Just don't get too badly gored by their wicked horns while you're out there!

Zeus: Psyche set out at once toward the sheeps' meadow. Scissors in her hand, she was just about to chase after a little lamb to give it a haircut when she heard a voice.

Reed: Don't try it, kid!

Psyche: Who said that?

Reed: Me. Down here, sticking out of the water right by your left foot.

Psyche: A reed?

Reed: You know, tall grass, loves shallow water—that's me!

Psyche: (startled) Now a piece of grass is telling me what I should do?

Reed: Those golden sheep will tear you apart in a second if you try to go near them.

Psyche: Then how am I supposed to get some of their wool?

Reed: They've been running through some brambles. When they're sleeping, run up to those thorn bushes and collect the bits of wool they've left hanging there. You'll get your wool without getting stuck.

Psyche: Thanks for the tip! I'll be more careful about where I walk from now on.

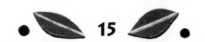

Zeus: Aphrodite was furious when Psyche returned with the golden wool. She gave the young beauty more horrible tasks to complete, but each time some plant or animal took pity on Psyche and lent her a hand. Finally, Aphrodite gave her an empty box.

Aphrodite: Here's your final task. Take this box down to the queen of the Underworld and bring back some of her beauty!

Zeus: Persephone, as you may know, is the queen of the Underworld—the place where all the dead go. It's not a place for live people, that's for sure. Well, Psyche managed to get by all the fierce and terrible guards down there, and into the court of the queen. She even convinced the queen to give up some of her beauty. Then the trouble started.

Psyche: Hmm, I wonder what Persephone's beauty secret is. . .Maybe it could help me, since these horrible assignments from Aphrodite have been really hard on my skin. . .

Zeus: She opened the box just a peep. Instantly, a foul, powerful wind rushed out of the crack and into her face.

Psyche: (gasping) Help! Help! I can't breathe!

Zeus: She fell to the ground, overpowered by the fumes that began forcing her back toward the Underworld for good. Luckily, Cupid appeared just at that moment.

Cupid: My mother knows how to lock a door, but she always forgets to lock the window! Psyche, I'm coming!

Zeus: He raced over to his bride, closed the dangerous box, and revived Psyche with his special godly powers.

Cupid: Just what has my mother been making you do?

Psyche: It's a long story. . .

Zeus: When Cupid heard how Psyche had worked to win him back, his love for her grew deeper than ever. As soon as he could, he brought her up to me, Zeus, and asked a special favor.

Cupid: Oh, king of the gods, please make my bride a god like the rest of us. I want her to be not only my bride but also my partner. She can help me with all the young lovers out there in the world.

Zeus: So I said, "So be it!" and gave Psyche a golden cup full of nectar, our special drink here on Mount Olympus. As soon as she took a sip, she became a goddess. That evening Olympus thundered and shook as we danced the night away. Even Aphrodite—who could hardly object to her son marrying another god—came and danced at the feast.

The End

FOR THE TEACHER

Talk About It

- What kind of a person is Psyche, judging from this play? Make a list of words that describe her.

- Does Aphrodite seem very god-like to you? Why or why not? Make a list of words that describe her.

- Why doesn't Cupid want Psyche to know who he is when they're married and living in the nice, big house? What are some examples of times when you might want to be known just for who you are, not for who your parents are and so on?

- How is Psyche helped by actions of the gods or luck? How is she hurt?

- Cupid promised Psyche that she could live "the good life"—with riches, a nice house, and a nice partner—as long as she never tried to see him. How hard would that promise be for you to live up to?

Extension Activities

- **Rewriting the Myth** Have groups of students brainstorm what this myth would be like if it were set in modern-times and made into a movie. Where might it take place? What kind of modern-day people/personalities would fit the characters of Aphrodite, Cupid and Psyche? How would the dialogue change? After they have finished brainstorming, challenge the groups to write a brief summary of what their movie would be like. Encourage them to include as many details as possible.

- **Dear Cupid** Divide the class into groups of four students. Have two students in each group write imaginary letters to Cupid, Psyche and/or Aphrodite asking advice on friendship or other matters. Then have the remaining two students reply, role-playing one, two, or all three of the characters. (Psyche, for example, probably wouldn't offer the same advice as Aphrodite.) Students might want to look at the "Dear Abby" feature in the local newspaper as a model, but you should read over any sample columns to check for appropriateness before giving them out to students.

- **Legacy** Challenge groups of students to research and produce collages that demonstrate the influence that Cupid and Aphrodite continue to have on life today (for example, the emphasis on physical beauty). Finished collages might include pictures from perfume or soap ads, or valentine candy and cards.

THE SOUND OF MUSIC GOES UNDERGROUND:

THE STORY OF ORPHEUS AND EURYDICE

In this myth a man named Orpheus uses his legendary musical skills to win the love of his life, Eurydice. After tragedy strikes, though, Orpheus goes where no living man has gone before in order to free his imprisoned wife. The place is the Underworld, and the only weapon he carries is his music.

Characters (in order of appearance)

Narrator 1

Narrator 2

Orpheus (OR-fee-us), singer and
    musician

Eurydice (yu-RID-uh-see), wife of
    Orpheus

Guest 1

Guest 2

Friend, friend of Orpheus

Charon (KAR-on), boatman of the
    Underworld

Sisyphus (SIS-ih-fus) (nonspeaking
    role), Underworld victim

Tantalos (TANT-ul-us) (nonspeaking
    role), Underworld victim

Hades (HAY-deez), king of the
    Underworld

Persephone (per-SEF-oh-nee), queen
    of the Underworld

Words to Watch For

Styx (stix), main river in the Underworld

Poseidon (puh-SIGH-dun), god of the sea

Cerberus (SER-bur-us), guard-dog of the
    Underworld

Demeter (di-MEET-ur), goddess of farming

Introduction

Narrator 1: The gods and goddesses of Greece loved music. They knew people loved it too. That's why one of their favorite humans was a man called Orpheus.

Narrator 2: He was such a good singer, and played his small harp so beautifully, that people stopped whatever they were doing when they heard him. Animals stopped right in their tracks when they caught just one of the notes he played. Flowers and trees turned away from the sun if it meant they could hear his music. Even rough seas were known to become calm at the sound of Orpheus' music-making.

Scene One: Sounds of Joy and Woe

Narrator 1: But even famous musicians get lonely. One day Orpheus married one of his biggest fans, a beautiful woman named Eurydice.

Orpheus: The music must be just right for our wedding today.

Eurydice: I'm sure whatever you play will be fantastic.

Orpheus: For you, my dear, it has to be the best I've ever done!

Narrator 2: And so they were married in a splendid, crowded festival. The bride and groom wore dazzling outfits. The food was delicious, and there was plenty of it. But the real treat of the day was the music.

Narrator 1: Orpheus played such sweet love songs to his bride that all the wedding guests were filled with joy. Young guests fell in love with their dates, if they weren't in love already. Older guests relived how they felt on their wedding days.

Narrator 2: No one wanted Orpheus to stop singing.

Orpheus: My voice is going. I'll be back after a short break. . .

Guest 1: (shouting) No, don't stop! Just one more song! Please!

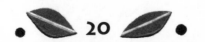

Guest 2: (shouting more loudly) No, just two more songs!

Narrator 1: Other people in the room started shouting. Shoving matches even broke out over song selections. The once-joyful crowd had become very grumpy indeed.

Eurydice: (to Orpheus) Darling, I can't stand this shouting and fighting. I'm going to get a breath of fresh air.

Orpheus: Good idea. Come back in a few minutes and I'll start playing again. That will quiet them all down.

Narrator 2: Eurydice walked out into a lovely, grassy meadow near the feast hall. As she pushed through the tall grass to reach a nearby stream, she thought about how lucky she was to be married to Orpheus.

Narrator 1: Suddenly, a horrible pain shot through her leg as if she had been knifed in the bottom of her foot. It was only then that Eurydice heard the terrible hissing sound and looked down to see a big, deadly snake pulling its head from her heel! Death would soon take this beautiful, unlucky bride down to the deep, dark kingdom of Hades: the Underworld.

Narrator 2: Back at the party, Orpheus was wondering what happened to Eurydice.

Orpheus: Where's my lovely bride? I want to sing a song I wrote just for her.

Guest 1: (rushing inside) Oh, Orpheus, something terrible has happened!

Narrator 1: Orpheus' blood ran cold, knowing from the look on the guest's face that something awful had happened to Eurydice.

Scene Two: A Dark Trip

Narrator 2: For days and weeks, Orpheus mourned the death of his bride. His sad songs brought tears to the eyes of everyone who lived within the sound of his playing. But then one day there was silence—silence because Orpheus was thinking. Thinking of how he could see Eurydice once more. . .

Orpheus: I can't stand this! I can't live without Eurydice. I'm going to find her.

Friend: Find her? What do you mean?

Orpheus: I'm going to the Underworld to bring her back!

Friend: Are you crazy? How are you going to fight Hades and all the spirits that help him rule the Underworld?

Orpheus: I'll use my music to bring Eurydice back.

Narrator 1: So Orpheus, armed only with his harp, set out to bring his bride back from the land of the dead. He went to a famous cave that led to the Underworld and entered it. Down, down, down he traveled. The tunnel became darker and darker, until he started to see the glimmer of a torch in the distance.

Narrator 2: He had come upon Charon, the boatman who carries spirits of the dead across the poisonous River Styx and into the kingdom of Hades.

Orpheus: Hello, I'm trying to get to Hades. Could you help me?

Charon: Where's your gold coin?

Orpheus: You mean, there's a fee to get in?

Charon: Of course. Greeks put a gold coin under the tongue of those who have died. I'm the one that collects those coins. Now pay up.

Orpheus: But, I'm not dead!

Charon: Sure, that's what they all say. You'll get used to it.

Orpheus: No, it's true. I'm a musician and I've come to take my wife back from the dead.

Charon: Forget about it! Do you know how much trouble I'd get in if Hades knew I let a living soul into his kingdom?

Orpheus: Maybe he would make an exception.

Charon: No way! He's a very touchy guy.

Orpheus: Why?

Charon: He and his brothers Zeus and Poseidon love to gamble. Once they were arguing over who controlled the different parts of the universe, so they decided to throw dice to settle the question. Zeus won big and got the Heavens. Poseidon got the Sea and the Land. Hades, the big loser, got stuck with the Underworld. He's been upset ever since.

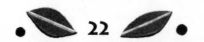

Narrator 1: Charon crossed his arms and wouldn't budge. After a few moments of tense silence, Orpheus took out his harp and began singing about a gently flowing river. The song charmed the crusty old boatman.

Charon: (softly) Your song reminds me of when I was a young man, just starting out in the boat business. (gruffly) Well, come along, then. I'll carry you across the river, but I warn you, you won't get past Cerberus on the other side.

Orpheus: Cerberus?

Charon: That's the three-headed dog that Hades keeps chained up at the entrance to his kingdom. He's got three sets of teeth to tear apart any trespassers.

Narrator 2: Even before they got to the far shore, Orpheus heard the fierce dog snarling at him. The dog's bark sounded three times meaner than the meanest dog in the Upper World.

Narrator 1: By the time Charon pulled up on shore, though, Orpheus knew what to do next. He made up a quick song about dogs—about puppies running through the fields and hunting dogs chasing rabbits through a forest.

Narrator 2: The beast stopped growling and started wagging his tail. Orpheus calmly passed through the gate and into Hades' kingdom. When Orpheus walked by Cerberus, he gave Orpheus a lick—or really, three licks from his three tongues.

Charon: Well, welcome to Hades' kingdom. I can't believe you've made it this far. Good luck getting your wife back. You're on your own now. . .

Orpheus: Please, wait a second. It's so dark here I can barely see. Who are those people up ahead ?

Charon: Those are spirits—people who died and now exist in the Underworld. They displeased the gods during their lives, so Hades has put them right up front to make an example out of them.

Orpheus: Who's that trying to move that huge rock?

Charon: His name is Sisyphus. His punishment is to push that rock up to the top of that steep hill. Getting that rock up there just once is no sweat. Listen to what Hades did to make it more difficult: Every time the rock gets near the top it rolls back down and Sisyphus has got to start all over again.

Orpheus: How long does he have to do that?

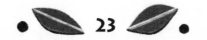

Charon: Only for forever. It's kind of a rocky job, ha ha. That's a bit of Underworld humor for you.

Orpheus: What about that guy over there, the one who's floating in that pond, right under those beautiful fruit trees?

Charon: That's Tantalos. Hades has made him always hungry and thirsty.

Orpheus: Why doesn't he just take a drink or grab a piece of fruit?

Charon: Watch. Every time he bends his head to take a sip of water, all the water disappears from the pond. When he reaches for an apple or a pear, the trees pull their branches away.

Orpheus: (nervously) Hey, what's that rumbling sound? It's getting louder and louder.

Charon: (dashing back fearfully toward his boat) That's Hades. He's heard you're in his kingdom and, by the sound of it, he's not very happy. Good luck, but don't tell him that I helped you! Goodbye!

Scene Three: Meeting the King

Narrator 1: Orpheus was alone. The rumbling grew louder. A great black storm cloud surrounded him. When the cloud cleared, Orpheus stood in chains in front of the thrones of Hades and Persephone, the king and queen of the Underworld.

Hades: What a rude spirit you are to come to my kingdom before I called you!

Orpheus: But I'm not a spirit! I'm still alive!

Hades: So you are. We can take care of that problem quite easily!

Narrator 2: Hades raised his scepter and was about to cast some terrible spell on Orpheus when the musician cried out.

Orpheus: Wait! Please, your highness, I've just come for my wife! She was killed on our wedding day. It must have been a mistake.

Hades: A mistake! Does anyone ever tell my brother Zeus that he made a mistake? Do people come bothering my brother Poseidon for favors? No! How come I have to deal with all the losers? Prepare for your fate!

Orpheus: Yes, your highness. But first. . .let me sing you a song.

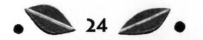

Narrator 1: Then Orpheus performed the most beautiful song of his career. His harp made sweet music as he sang about his love for Eurydice. When he described her beauty, Sisyphus stopped rolling his rock and didn't care when the boulder went crashing backward. Tantalos forgot about his hunger and thirst.

Narrator 2: The song moved the king, though he didn't want anyone to notice.

Hades: Well, I, uh. . .(gruffly) Musician, your song has entertained us. We don't get many road shows down here. I'm prepared to give you an easy punishment for the rest of eternity. Now, you'll have to swallow an ocean and. . .

Orpheus: No, your highness. I'm sorry but I can't stay. I want to bring Eurydice back to the land of the living.

Hades: Why, you ungrateful little bug! Forget about that easy sentence I was going to give you.

Narrator 1: Just then, Persephone spoke up. Her face was covered with dark veils but Orpheus could tell she was beautiful. Her voice was strong but gentle.

Persephone: Wait, dear. I know that song touched you. Please consider this human's request. Show everyone that you can be more merciful than your crude brothers Zeus and Poseidon.

Hades: They are quite crude, aren't they? Zeus throws thunderbolts all over whenever he gets angry. Poseidon causes tidal waves and drowns sailors when he's cranky.

Persephone: What about letting Eurydice go?

Hades: But, if I let one spirit go, all the spirits would want to go back. We'd be rulers of an empty kingdom.

Persephone: Make an exception this one time, in the name of love.

Hades: Love?

Persephone: It's not such a big word. You should know it! Remember how madly you loved me? Cupid must have sent an arrow right to your heart.

Narrator 2: Even Orpheus knew the story of how Persephone had become Hades' wife. Once, when Hades was spying on the Upper World, he had fallen in love with Persephone. He kidnapped her and brought her home, enraging Persephone's mother, Demeter. Demeter—the goddess of farming—went on strike, refusing to allow any crops to grow until she got her daughter back.

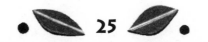

Narrator 1: Things got so bad on earth that Zeus had to step in and make a deal. Persephone would spend half the year with her mother, and half the year with Hades. As a result, Greeks say, when Persephone is with her mother, humans enjoy spring and summer. When her daughter is with Hades, though, Demeter shuts down all planting and harvesting, and earth moves into the seasons of fall and winter.

Scene Four: The Bargain

Narrator 2: Persephone's argument in defense of Orpheus won the king over.

Hades: Yes, my dear, you're right again. We'll let this singer have his bride back. After all, everyone makes mistakes. Listen, Orpheus. You may have your bride back on one condition. You must not look at her until you both enter the light of the Upper World. Is that clear?

Orpheus: Of course, great king!

Hades: Then turn and start your journey home right now, before I change my mind. Eurydice will walk right behind you. But remember, don't turn around!

Narrator 1: Orpheus followed the king's orders. At first he wondered if Hades had tricked him. Was there really anyone behind him? He was about to turn around to check when he heard light footsteps behind him.

Narrator 2: He retraced his steps past Cerberus. The dog had never seen anyone except Persephone leave the Underworld. Now he saw a human and a spirit leave together. He turned his three heads to the side and barked three times in confusion.

Narrator 1: Then Orpheus saw Charon, unloading a fresh boatload of spirits in the Underworld. Orpheus walked right into the boat and sat in front, leaving plenty of room for Eurydice to sit down behind him.

Charon: Return trips from the dead! Now I've seen everything. What's next? Tour groups?

Narrator 2: By the time they reached the far shore, Orpheus was in actual pain, waiting to see his wife.

Orpheus: This trip is taking forever! I don't think I can stand it!

Narrator 1: As they climbed up through the dark cave taking them back to the Upper World, the singer's mind started to play tricks on him.

Orpheus: I hope that Hades gave me the right spirit. What if there were two spirits named Eurydice? Maybe I should just peek to make sure there's been no mistake. No, no, I'm going to keep my promise.

Narrator 2: Higher and higher they climbed. With each step Orpheus found it more difficult to keep from turning to look at the spirit behind him.

Orpheus: Eurydice is the love of my life. Imagine what it will be like to hug her again! To kiss her! My loneliness will be ended!

Narrator 1: Soon, he could see the light of the Upper World at the top of the cave. Their journey was almost over.

Orpheus: I can't stand it any longer. We're just. . .about. . .THERE!

Narrator 2: As he was just about to burst into the sunlight, Orpheus turned around. Just a step behind him, still in the dark shadows of the cave, he saw his beautiful wife. She looked at him with loving eyes. . .

Narrator 1: She was like a beautiful picture, but then suddenly the color began to vanish, leaving only a black and white outline. Then, the black lines became fainter and fainter, until they too were almost gone.

Orpheus: Wait, Eurydice, this was just a mistake. It was only a peek!

Narrator 2: He tried to throw his arms around the fading image, but his arms passed through air, leaving the singer hugging only himself.

Narrator 1: Desperately, Orpheus went back down the cave to try to enter the Underworld once more. He played his lyre for Charon the boatman yet again, but this time it didn't work.

Charon: I'm sorry. I'm under strict orders from the boss. He says he gave you and Eurydice a second chance. There are no third chances in the Underworld.

Scene Five: The Conclusion

Narrator 2: Alone and heartbroken, Orpheus made the long climb back to the Upper World. When he arrived, he had no interest in music or anything else.

Narrator 1: But gradually, Orpheus did start playing again. His group of admirers began growing to its old size—though everyone noticed that all his songs were now sad and lonely-sounding.

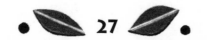

Narrator 2: It was a sad ending for the once-happy musician, but it did have a bright side. When it came time for Orpheus to cross over to the Underworld for good, Charon gave him a free boat ride. Cerberus barked three times and wagged his tail. Most importantly, Orpheus was reunited with his beloved Eurydice. And they say his music made the sorrows of the Underworld that much easier to bear for Sisyphus, Tantalos and all the other spirits.

The End

FOR THE TEACHER

Talk About It

- What effect does Orpheus' playing have on his listeners? What kind of music has that effect on you? Why do you think music can be so powerful?

- According to this myth, why do we have the four seasons of the year? Why does this explanation make sense, in the setting of this story?

- What kind of a god is Hades? How is his behavior affected by the way he gets along, or doesn't get along, with his brothers? How is life in the Underworld different from life in the Upper World?

- If you were Eurydice, how would you describe what life is like, living under the gods of Greece? Is life fair? Why or why not? Do the gods mean for it to be fair?

Extension Activities

- **Rewrite the Myth** Challenge students to rewrite this myth from the point of view of Eurydice, moving the setting up to modern times. (The cave to the Underworld might be a subway tunnel, for example, and Charon might have to ferry people across a radioactive waste-site rather than the poisonous River Styx.) Discuss whether changing the ending to a more happy one (in which Eurydice survives) would be a bit far-fetched in the traditional Greek world. What god or goddess could they call to their aid to make the ending a happy one?

- **Name That Tune** Encourage students to prepare a short report on one of their favorite songs that makes them feel peaceful and full of hope. Students should write a paragraph describing why they think the music (its rhythms and/or words) makes them feel those emotions. Encourage them to tape an excerpt of their song and play it for the class, if possible.

- **Legacy** Challenge groups of students to survey their parents, grandparents, relatives, teachers and/or neighbors regarding the songs or musical pieces that make them feel relaxed and peaceful. When students conduct their interviews they should write down the titles of the songs; the names of the songs' performers and/or composers; and roughly when the music was written and/or was popular. Groups should choose a format in which to present their information (for example, collage, with images of instruments used or groups performing; or perhaps sound collage, recording excerpts of music, prefaced with brief identifications of the piece and to whom it is meaningful).

RANSOM:

THE STORY OF THESEUS AND THE MINOTAUR

In this myth a prince named Theseus risks his own life to stop the deadly payment of human lives that his father is forced to make to a cruel enemy. To win his gamble, Theseus will have to overcome the Minotaur, a raging, human-eating bull, as well as the depths of the deep blue sea.

Characters (in order of appearance)

Narrator 1
Narrator 2
Messenger
Aegeus (ee-JEE-us), king of Athens
Theseus (THEE-see-us), prince of Athens

Captives (nonspeaking roles)
Minos (MY-nus), king of Crete
Sailor
Mermaid
Ariadne (AIR-ee-AD-nee), the princess of Crete

Words to Watch For
Crete (KREET), Greek island south of Athens
Minotaur (MIN-uh-tawr), powerful animal
Labyrinth (LAB-uh-rinth), huge maze

Introduction

Narrator 1: On the island of Crete lived a cruel and powerful king by the name of Minos. People all over the Greek world feared his army and navy, and paid the heavy fees Minos demanded just to be left alone. The people of Athens had to pay an especially heavy price. Minos' son had died on a visit to Athens, so Minos made Athens pay "blood money" to make sure that this tragic event would never be forgotten.

Narrator 2: Every nine years the king of Athens—Aegeus—had to send seven young men and seven young women to Crete. Choosing those fourteen youths was agony, because everyone knew what their horrible fate would be. In exchange for peace for the rest of Athens, those unlucky victims would be taken to Crete and fed to a deadly creature owned by King Minos. Its name was the Minotaur.

Narrator 1: The Minotaur had the head of a human but the body of a bull. It was huge and powerful and lived on a diet of humans that it hunted down. Because it was so deadly, Minos kept the Minotaur in a massive maze called "the Labyrinth" to make sure it never, ever escaped.

Narrator 2: The victims from Athens were brought to the Labyrinth one by one and left there until the Minotaur found them. Lost and confused, they never knew when they would meet their fate. No one ever escaped.

Scene One: The Palace in Athens

Messenger: Your time is up. King Minos says that you must be prepared to give him your next batch of youths when he arrives tomorrow. He says that if you're slow in choosing them, he will destroy Athens and take even more victims himself.

Aegeus: (sad and confused) Is there no way out of this terrible bargain? To save our city we must send our children to their deaths. But there's no choice. Quickly, we must hold a lottery and choose who must go to Crete.

Theseus: Father, wait. We can't just send those people off to die! Why, they're the same age that I am. We've got to do something!

Aegeus: No, my son. As long as the Minotaur lives and Minos keeps demanding his ransom, there is no way out.

Theseus: Then send me as one of the fourteen! I know that I can defeat that evil beast and put a stop to Minos' cruel game.

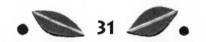

Aegeus: Sending these young people to their deaths is bad enough for me. If I lose you too, my heart would break. Then Athens would be without its king and its prince.

Theseus: But I can win. With the gods on my side, I won't fail you or our people.

Narrator 1: The king saw something in his son's eyes that gave him hope. He knew that the gods loved his son and would watch over him, so he let him go as one of the victims. Instead of wearing his royal robes, Theseus put on the simple white tunic worn by the other thirteen youths. He also left behind the royal ring his father had given him. Now no one would know he was the king's son.

Aegeus: Theseus, I want you to take these white sails with you. If you succeed in your mission, hoist the white sails on your ship instead of the black sails that our sailors normally use. I'll watch the sea every day and pray that I see your white sails heading toward home.

Scene Two: The Journey to Crete

Narrator 2: The next day King Minos arrived to collect the victims. He gloated as the youths, including Theseus, were led onto his ship. Though Theseus stood tall, his companions wept as they left their friends and family, expecting never to see them again. The trip to Crete was dark and gloomy—but not for Minos. He enjoyed hearing the victims' sobs and mocked them when he felt like it.

Minos: (speaking to the captives) My pet is very hungry. It's been nine years since he's had some Athenians over for dinner. You'll make a splendid fourteen-course meal for my bullish friend.

Theseus: Watch out, King Minos. The gods will punish you for putting us through this torture.

Minos: Oh, a rebel?

Theseus: I know the gods are on the side of right—that is, on our side.

Minos: Oh, really? Let's check the score so far. You were chosen by lottery to become a human sacrifice. You were abandoned by family and friends and given a one-way ride to the bullpen of a man-eating monster. Look at me, on the other hand. I'm a rich and powerful king. Hmm, I wonder whose side the gods are on?

Theseus: It's true you've had your fun, but soon it's going to be over.

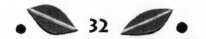

Narrator 1: Minos could see that this bold fellow was getting his crew nervous. He knew that, with all the talk about the gods, it would look bad to kill Theseus right there. But Minos always had an evil scheme when he needed one.

Minos: Enough already with this talk! We'll have a little test that will prove whether the gods are really interested in helping you. I'll drop one of my rings in the ocean. If the gods favor you, you'll dive in and bring my ring right back.

Theseus: That's a deal.

Narrator 2: Minos took a plain-looking ring off his finger and threw it into the sea. Like a shot, Theseus dove off the side of the ship to retrieve it.

Minos: (shouting to his crew) Set all the sails! Let's get this ship moving!

Sailor: But your highness, shouldn't we wait for that youth to come back up? He'll never be able to catch up with our ship. We'd be leaving him here to drown.

Minos: Oh really? What a pity that would be. (to the crew) Anyone who doesn't obey my orders will be an appetizer for the Minotaur. Set all the sails!

Narrator 1: Under the waves, Theseus began to regret his boldness. His lungs were ready to burst and the sea was cold and dark. How could he ever find that ring?

Narrator 2: But the gods did not forget Theseus. Just when it seemed he couldn't last any longer, Theseus found that he could breathe underwater. Then he felt two things brush by on either side of him. Sharks! his mind screamed. But they were dolphins, friendly dolphins who had come to be his guides. Theseus grabbed hold of their fins and they pulled him farther and farther into the watery deep. At last, they reached the realm of the mermaids.

Narrator 1: Their caves at the bottom of the sea were filled with gold and silver treasures taken from sunken ships. One mermaid swam up to Theseus with King Minos' ring already in her hand.

Mermaid: It's not such a beautiful ring. I can't see why you came all this way just to get it. But, here, you can have it.

Narrator 2: After that, the dolphins pulled Theseus on to Crete—ahead of Minos' ship—so he was there to greet the king when the ship arrived. Minos was shocked, but said nothing except to order Theseus back with the other victims.

Minos: Chain him up with all the others and take them to the palace dungeon. If the gods are really on his side, they'll save him from the Minotaur. No one else can!

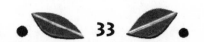

Narrator 1: Ariadne, Minos' daughter, watched from her palace window as the victims trudged to the prison where they would be held until they were placed in the Labyrinth.

Ariadne: I wonder who that fellow is in front of the line. He seems so brave for someone who's about to die. Oh, why does my father do these horrible things!

Narrator 2: She fell in love with Theseus at first sight and promised herself that she would not let him die like all the others. Perhaps he could even help her escape from her evil father.

Scene Three: The Plan

Narrator 1: While the guards were sleeping, Ariadne crept to the cell where Theseus was being held.

Ariadne: (whispering) Wake up, but don't make a sound!

Theseus: (whispering back) Did the king send you to torment me?

Ariadne: No. I'm Minos' daughter, but I want to help save you from the Minotaur.

Theseus: Is this some kind of a trick?

Ariadne: Listen to me. No matter how brave you are, you'll die without my help. Even if the Minotaur doesn't kill you, you'll be trapped in the Labyrinth forever. Here, take this ball of string. Once they shut you inside the Labyrinth, tie this end of the string to the doorway. When you move around inside, pull the string with you. Then, if you're successful and you defeat the Minotaur, you can follow it back to safety.

Theseus: But how can I find the beast before it finds me?

Ariadne: The Minotaur is lazy. It thinks it can find its victims any time it wants. It sleeps late. You must find it while it's sleeping and surprise it. That's your only hope of winning.

Theseus: What can I do to repay you for your help?

Ariadne: Help me escape from this island. I can't stand my father and his wicked ways.

Theseus: It's a deal. When I leave this island with my friends from Athens, we'll take you with us.

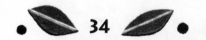

Scene Four: The Battle

Narrator 2: The next day a smiling and singing Minos visited the young Athenians in prison.

Minos: Well, the time has come for the Minotaur to be fed. Any volunteers for the first round?

Theseus: Let me be first. I think the gods will protect me.

Minos: I couldn't have picked a better candidate. (to the guards) Bring him to the Labyrinth at dawn tomorrow. Let's start fourteen days of feasting to celebrate our little agreement with Athens!

Narrator 1: Theseus was brought to the entrance of the maze just before sunrise the next day. There he stopped and turned to address Minos one more time before entering.

Theseus: This bloodshed will end and Athens will no longer feed the Minotaur.

Narrator 2: Then he was shoved inside the maze, and a door slammed behind him. Though others victims had to be forced at sword-point into its scary paths, Theseus seemed almost glad to be entering the Labyrinth.

Minos: (to himself) I must say, I've never seen such a willing sacrifice. What a relief! Now that that troublemaker is gone, I'm sure the others will give me no problem.

Narrator 1: Theseus didn't forget what Ariadne had told him. He had hidden the string under his clothes. While speaking to Minos, he had secretly attached the end of the string to the maze's doorway. Now he was ready to move inside.

Narrator 2: Following the low rumble of the Minotaur's snores, Theseus stumbled ahead as quickly as he could until he was near the beast. As he inched closer, the Minotaur opened its eyes and jumped up.

Narrator 1: They fought a fierce battle. With his bare hands Theseus grabbed the Minotaur. The animal's power was enormous, and it was a miracle that Theseus was able to hold his own, let alone get the better of the beast. The deadly showdown finally came to an end when Theseus killed the horrible beast. He thanked the gods for their help.

Narrator 2: Following Ariadne's string back through the maze, Theseus was able to find the path back to freedom.

Theseus: Ariadne, I've won!

Ariadne: I want to believe it, but I still can't. How did you get past the guards at the entrance to the Labyrinth?

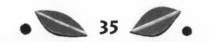

Theseus: They were asleep when I came out. I guess they never expected anyone to walk out alive. Quick, let's get the rest of the Athenians and get out of here! We've got to get away from this island before anyone catches on!

Narrator 1: So they gathered the other Athenians together and sailed for Athens. But the gods, who had supported Theseus before, now sent bad luck his way.

Narrator 2: A storm forced the ship to land on a deserted island. Ariadne was the first to go ashore. Just as she reached shore, though, a powerful gust of wind drove the ship far out to sea again. By the time Theseus was able to force his way back to the island, Ariadne had died, probably of a broken heart.

Narrator 1: No one knows exactly what happened. What god could have wanted such a terrible thing to take place? Only this much was clear. When Theseus set sail for Athens once again, he was so upset by Ariadne's death that he completely forgot to change his ship's sails, as he had promised his father. His ship sailed on, with black sails instead of the white ones he had promised to use.

Aegeus: (looking out of his tower) A ship. . .I see a ship coming from Crete! It looks like the ship that carried my son away. Let its sails be white!

Narrator 2: When the old king saw that the ship had black sails, his heart broke and he collapsed in grief, falling from his tower into the sea. From then on, that sea was called by his name. Today we still call it the Aegean Sea.

Narrator 1: All of Athens rejoiced that the captives had been brought home alive and that the Minotaur had been killed. But Theseus couldn't celebrate that day. He had lost not only Ariadne, but his father as well. It was with a heavy heart that he became Athens' new king and began a brilliant career that, some would say, would bring democracy to the land of Greece.

The End

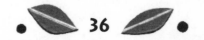

FOR THE TEACHER

Talk About It

- Should King Aegeus have given the captives to Minos? What else could he have done? What kinds of no-win situations have you or people you know faced? What does it take to get through those kinds of situations?

- How would you describe Greek gods and goddesses, based just on what they do or don't do in this play? Back up your descriptions with examples from this play.

- It can be said that there are two heroes in this story: Theseus and Ariadne. Why might that be so? What makes a person a hero?

Extension Activities

- **The Lottery** The unlucky Athenian captives sent to feed the Minotaur were chosen by lottery. To demonstrate what it is like to be chosen purely by chance, try setting up a lottery system in your class to pick the Minotaur's "victims." Ask students if the lottery is a good device for making choices. Remind students that we have used the lottery system in our country not only as a way to select prize winners but also as a method of choosing people to be sent to war. Should important decisions be made by chance? Ask them to write a short essay describing other ways of making choices. Older students may want to read Shirley Jackson's famous short story, "The Lottery," for more context.

- **Designing Minds** Challenge student groups to get ready to design the basic outline of an imaginary interactive game based on this myth. The goal of this "game" will be to allow players to make their own choices—and experience the resulting consequences—that shape the story. (For example, they could choose not to hand over fourteen new victims. As a result, though, Minos sacks Athens. Then the city will have new choices to make.) To start, familiarize students with the concept of a flow chart and how it works. Then encourage groups to brainstorm all the points in the story when choices can be made, and what the possible consequences could be of each choice. Final products could be designed in poster-size, with accompanying illustrations, and groups could "play" each other's posters. Discuss how different the myth's plot and resolution could be, if different choices were made along the way.

- **Legacy** Challenge student groups to put together a collage or exhibit that reflects the enduring influences of mermaids, terrifying monsters that are at least part-human and maze-based adventures in today's world. Movies, tuna cans and computer games are all potential mining sites for this activity.

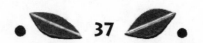

FLYING HIGH (AND ITS DANGERS):

THE STORY OF DAEDALUS AND ICARUS

In this myth we learn about Daedalus and Icarus, the legendary father-son team who first tested human flight with homemade wings. Daedalus, the great inventor and caring father, hadn't always been so caring. Or do all heroes have their faults?

Characters (in order of appearance)

Narrator 1
Narrator 2
Polycasta (polly-CAST-uh), Daedalus' sister
Daedalus (DED-ul-us), an inventor
Carpenter
Talos (TAL-us), Daedalus' nephew

Athena (uh-THEE-nuh), goddess of wisdom
Minos (MY-nos), king of Crete
Guard
Icarus (IK-uh-rus), his son
Fisherman
Shepherd

Words to Watch For
Sicily (SIS-uh-lee), Italian island west of Greece

Introduction

Narrator 1: Once a man named Daedalus lived in Athens—the Greek city whose protector was Athena, the goddess of wisdom. One day Daedalus was making a statue of Athena, and the goddess liked it so much she decided to give him special powers. Thanks to her he became Athens' top inventor and builder. Everyone admired his cleverness at making gadgets, and his ability to solve problems that had baffled people for years. Even Aegeus, the king of Athens at the time, counted on Daedalus for advice about new buildings and special projects.

Narrator 2: But it wasn't enough for Daedalus to be the greatest inventor in Athens. He wanted to be the only inventor in Athens. He couldn't stand anyone else getting recognition. The great inventor even became worried that his own nephew, his apprentice, would steal some of his glory.

Scene One: The Fall

Narrator 1: In Athens, Daedalus' reputation as a wise man and clever inventor was growing. He soaked up praise from others, especially his family members.

Polycasta: (looking at building plans her brother made) Who would have thought it? I hate to admit it—after all those fights we had as kids—but my own brother is a genius.

Daedalus: Sister, you look like you ate something that didn't agree with you.

Polycasta: No, brother, it's not my lunch. I'm just remembering that mother always spoiled you. And then Athena sharpened your brain like a pencil. Some people get all the luck.

Daedalus: Now don't get upset, just because I'm famous and you're not. My ideas will help our whole city. And if I can ever do you a favor, please let me know.

Polycasta: I was hoping you'd say that! My son, Talos, loves to build things around the house. He built a doghouse that is so comfortable, the dog refuses to come out. Then he made a mousetrap that's so attractive, mice have been lining up to try it out. Please, take him on as your apprentice. Teach him something useful and keep him out of my hair.

Daedalus: I don't really need anyone right now. . .

Polycasta: He'll work for free. You must need someone to clean up around here. Someone to take out the garbage? Surely Athena didn't give you a special talent for that!

Daedalus: All right, all right. Having a kid like him around will allow me more time for my important work. He can start tomorrow. But he must remember that I'm very busy with very important people, so he needs to stay out of my way.

Narrator 2: So Talos, a youth about twelve years old, came to stay with his uncle Daedalus. At first, he quietly went about his chores in the inventor's shop. He cleaned up the tools, washed all the dishes and took out the rubbish.

Narrator 1: One day, an Athenian came to the shop to ask Daedalus' help. Talos was sweeping up in the corner.

Carpenter: I need a tool that can cut through wood quickly and neatly. Chopping wood with an ax is too messy and takes too long. Can you help?

Daedalus: Maybe if you used a bigger ax, or a spear. . .Hmm. . .Let me think about it. Come back in a day or two and I'll have something for you.

Narrator 2: When the man left, Talos spoke up.

Talos: Uncle, look at this drawing I made. It's a plan for a tool I call a "saw." It will cut through wood more easily than an ax.

Daedalus: Hmm. . .How does it work?

Talos: See these sharp parts here that look like teeth? They cut right through the wood when you move the teeth back and forth across the wood. I came up with the idea one day when I was emptying the garbage. I saw a fish skeleton and it made me think . . .

Daedalus: Shhh! Didn't I tell you not to disturb my thinking? Give me that silly drawing and go back to your chores!

Narrator 1: But Daedalus didn't throw away the "silly drawing." He used Talos' idea to make a saw out of metal. Then he brought it to the carpenter.

Carpenter: How did you think of this. . .this "saw," as you call it? You really are clever!

Daedalus: Oh, it just came to me one night. . .as I was taking out the garbage.

Narrator 2: Daedalus took the all credit but Talos wasn't discouraged. He felt that some-day his uncle would recognize his talent.

Talos: Look at what I've made, Uncle. I call it a "compass." You can use it to draw perfect diagrams and to measure things exactly.

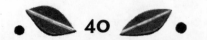

Daedalus: Give me that, and stop fooling around! You've got work to do! (to himself) I've got to do something about this boy before I become the "second-best" inventor in Athens.

Narrator 1: That night Daedalus couldn't sleep, he was so angry and jealous. Finally he thought up a plan that made him feel better. He jumped out of bed and rushed over to Talos' room.

Daedalus: Talos, I was too harsh with you today. Forgive me. Come with me now, though. I'd like you to help me on a project right now. It's very important—on top of Athena's temple. I could use your advice.

Talos: Wow, that would be great! But. . .way up there? Right now, in the middle of the night, when it's so dark?

Daedalus: This shouldn't take long.

Narrator 2: When they got to the roof of the temple, Daedalus carried out his evil plot.

Daedalus: I've been asked to build a statue for that side of the tower. Lean over the edge and tell me if you think it's possible.

Talos: Well, it sure looks dangerous, but if you say so. . .

Narrator 1: As Talos leaned over, Daedalus gave him a swift push which sent the youth hurtling toward the paving stones. But before he hit the ground he quickly flapped his arms and miraculously began to move skyward.

Narrator 2: You see, Athena had watched the plot unfold and stepped in. In a flash, she turned Talos into a bird—a partridge, to be exact—and so spared his life. Then she had a few words with her former favorite.

Athena: You are a very sick man, Daedalus. I'm tempted to take back all the powers I've given you, but I won't. Instead, I'm going to banish you from Athens. You must wander through the world, praying that someone will take you in. Fate will have other punishments in store for you.

Scene Two: Rise and Downfall

Narrator 1: Daedalus wandered about, sailing from country to country, until he came to the island of Crete, where the evil king Minos was looking for a great inventor. Daedalus was hired on the spot and he soon settled down, married and had a son. The boy's name was Icarus, and Daedalus loved him very, very much.

Narrator 2: Now after years of working for Minos, Daedalus was given the job of designing the Labyrinth that would house Minos' meanest pet, the Minotaur. (For those of you who don't know, the Labyrinth is a maze and the Minotaur was a powerful creature that was killed by an Athenian named Theseus in the story before this one.) But when Theseus escaped from the Labyrinth, taking Minos' daughter Ariadne with him, someone was going to have to take the heat from Minos. That person was Daedalus.

Minos: Guards, bring the inventor to me.

Narrator 1: The palace guards brought in Daedalus, his hands bound behind him. A few steps behind the inventor, also bound, stood his son, Icarus.

Minos: What should I do with you? Theseus killed the Minotaur and escaped from the Labyrinth. Only you could have helped him do that. To make matters worse, he's run off with dear Ariadne.

Guard: Should we execute them now, your highness?

Minos: No! I've just thought of a fit punishment. Take the inventor and his son to the center of the maze and leave them there, without food or water. We'll let the inventor be trapped by his own invention!

Narrator 2: Daedalus' face became a mask of terror. When he had made the Labyrinth, even he got lost in the maze unless he had his master plans with him.

Daedalus: (thinking only about his son) I have one request, your highness. My son is afraid of the dark. Can we please have a supply of candles to take with us, so at least his last hours will be a little less frightening.

Minos: Very well, have your candles. That way, you'll be able to see each other starve.

Scene Three: In the Maze

Narrator 1: Daedalus and Icarus were blindfolded, brought to the center of the maze and set free. The guards retraced their steps, keeping the inventor and his son in their place by threatening them with arrows and spears.

Icarus: Father, what will we do? I'm already hungry. You must think of some way out of this.

Daedalus: I'm thinking as fast as I can, son. But even if we escape from this maze, Minos' army will catch us. If we make it to the sea, the king's navy will capture our ship before we're a mile from shore.

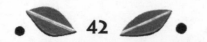

Narrator 2: Daedalus stayed awake all that night. He had just about given up hope when the chirping of birds signaled that the sun was about to rise.

Daedalus: You would have to be a bird to escape from Minos. . .That's it! Wake up, my son. We've got work to do!

Icarus: What? Father, have you gone crazy?

Daedalus: Just listen to me. Remember those bird calls I taught you? Use them now. Call down as many birds as you can. Quickly!

Narrator 1: Icarus made sounds that imitated the calls of blackbirds, seagulls and other birds. Hearing the calls, the birds swooped down toward the inventor and his son in the maze. The two quickly snatched as many feathers as they could. The lucky birds lost only a few feathers each.

Daedalus: Now, if we use the wax from the candles to hold the feathers like this. . .

Icarus: Father, please tell me what you're making.

Daedalus: I'm making wings! With these feathers and wax, I'm making wings that will carry us out of this maze and away from this island. Minos may control the land and the sea, but he doesn't rule the sky. We'll fly away!

Narrator 2: In just a day, Daedalus made sets of wings for himself and his son. Then they practiced with the wings until they knew they could fly.

Daedalus: Before we go, pay attention to my words, Icarus. Fly right behind me, do you hear? Don't fly too low, or the spray from the sea will wet your wings and pull you down. But don't fly too high either. If you fly too close to the sun, the wax that keeps the wings together will melt and you'll fall into the sea.

Icarus: Father, I promise I'll obey you.

Narrator 1: The two set out at the break of day. They flapped above the walls of the Labyrinth, and out over Minos' kingdom. The people below didn't know what to think about what they saw in the early morning sky.

Fisherman: That's the strangest pair of birds I've ever seen.

Shepherd: No, it must be two gods, visiting Earth.

Fisherman: I think I'd better go back to sleep.

Narrator 2: Once they were away from Minos' island, Daedalus and his son whooped and shouted.

Icarus: We're free as birds!

Daedalus: Just remember what I told you. Be careful!

Icarus: It feels great to fly! Gliding, soaring. Look at this dive I can do—and look how high I can go!

Daedalus: (alarmed) This is no time for fooling around, son. Stay close behind me. We've got to get to land as soon as we can.

Narrator 1: When his father's back was turned, Icarus spread his wings and soared as high as he could. He felt the rays of the sun warming his body. He let the currents of air take him even higher, just as a the tide will sometimes carry a swimmer deeper and deeper.

Icarus: (to himself) I'll catch up with my father in a second. After being in that cold Labyrinth, it's great to be flying. The sun feels so good.

Narrator 2: But something began to go terribly wrong. Icarus' wings began to get heavier and heavier. He started to feel melting wax warming his arms. When the boy turned to look to see what was happening, he saw a feather drop from his wings. Now he remembered what his father had said.

Icarus: Oh, no! Father, help me!

Narrator 1: But the boy was far behind and his voice could not reach his father's ears.

Narrator 2: Before long, hundreds of feathers were falling from the wings and Icarus was dropping fast to the blue sea below. He waved his arms frantically but it did no good.

Narrator 1: Flying ahead, Daedalus was lost in thought.

Daedalus: Now, if I could build wings for an entire army, that would be something. We could fly back to Crete and surprise Minos. I could be king. Icarus, how long do you think it would take me to. . .

Narrator 2: Turning around, he saw that he was alone in the beautiful cloudless sky. His heart pounded as he circled back, then saw what he feared most: Icarus floating lifeless in the sea.

Narrator 1: Daedalus landed on the first island he saw and convinced the fishermen there to bring back the body of his son. He buried Icarus on that island.

Narrator 2: As he said goodbye to his son, he noticed a bird sitting on a branch of the tree overlooking the grave. It was a partridge—the kind of bird his nephew Talos had become when Daedalus pushed him off the temple of Athena so many years before. At last, Daedalus understood how wrong and cruel that plan had been, now that his own son's life had been taken from him.

Narrator 1: For the rest of his life, it is said, Daedalus lived quietly on the island of Sicily, making toys for the children there. He easily could have won fame and fortune if he had built on his flying ideas, but the death of his son caused the inventor to hang up his wings—and his desire for fame—forever.

The End

FOR THE TEACHER

Talk About It

- Daedalus seems almost like two different people in this story. What is he like in the first part of the story? The second part? What helps to make him change so much?

- Daedalus is a brilliant inventor who saves his own life, and almost his son's, from an unfair death sentence. But he is also a murderer. Can he be considered a hero in any way, given the terrible crime he committed? Can imperfect people still be heroes?

- Icarus seems to have picked up at least one habit from his father—that is, he likes to do things his way. That pride leads to his downfall. Is it really possible that children can inherit parts of their personality from their parents? Why or why not?

Extension Activities

- **Rewrite the Myth** Challenge pairs of students to write a new version of the Daedalus/Icarus story, putting a new twist of their own choosing to it. (for example, set it in a different place, a different time, or with different technology; tell it from Talos' point of view, or his mother's, etc.) Encourage students to include as much detail as possible in their stories. Afterwards, have volunteers share and compare their stories.

- **Taking Flight** Encourage students to investigate early humans' fascination with flight and the ways they tried to make such dreams reality. (In China, for example, inventors created kites that could carry humans; early Peruvians may have developed some of the world's first hot-air balloons; and Leonardo da Vinci spent many hours studying bird anatomy in the hope of developing a wing system that would allow humans to soar through the air.) Advanced readers may wish to consult *Ancient Inventions*, by Peter James and Nick Thorpe (Ballantine, 1994), for information about early kites and balloons. A bit of information about da Vinci's research is contained in the CD-ROM *Leonardo: the Inventor* (Future Vision Multimedia, 1995).

- **Legacy** In the spirit of Daedalus and Talos, encourage students to brainstorm a list of inventions they feel they couldn't live without. Have groups of students investigate the origins of one of the inventions listed, and write a brief article summarizing their research. Later, after groups have shared their findings with the class, lead a discussion about the potential pitfalls of each invention for users. (Remind them that just as flight offered Icarus new freedom and fun, it also posed deadly risks if he wasn't careful.)

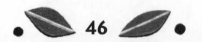

VANITY FAIR:

THE STORY OF ECHO AND NARCISSUS

In this myth, the lives of a chatty forest spirit and a self-centered young man meet in the heart of a forest. The result is filled with echoes, daffodil-like flowers—and a stern warning about the dangers of falling in love with yourself, or with someone who is similarly vain.

Characters (in order of appearance)

Narrator 1

Narrator 2

Hera (HERE-uh), queen of the gods

Zeus, king of the gods

Echo, a forest sprite, or fairy

Narcissus (nar-SIS-us), a young man

Nemesis (NEM-uh-sis), goddess of "pay-back" justice

Scene One: Not a Word!

Narrator 1: On Mount Olympus, the home of the gods, Zeus and Hera were having a very heated conversation about one of their forest sprites, or fairies.

Narrator 2: Those are beings that aren't nearly as powerful as gods, but have more powers than the average human.

Hera: I just can't stand it anymore. Something's got to be done!

Zeus: Well, have you tried to talk to her about it?

Hera: Talk to her! That's the whole problem. I can't even get a word in edgewise when she's around. She doesn't even give me a chance to talk to myself!

Zeus: Would you like me to have a word with—

Hera: It won't work! I've tried everything. I'm afraid that I'm going to lose my temper and. . .and. . .you know what that means!

Zeus: Now, now. I know what you're thinking. Don't even think about using one of my thunderbolts. We've got to settle this peacefully. You've got to. . .negotiate with her.

Narrator 1: They were talking about Echo, one of Zeus' sprites that was supposed to serve Hera. Indeed, Echo was a good servant, but she had one problem. She couldn't stop talking.

Echo: (speaking to some other sprites) Listen, did you hear who was turned into a tree? Well, the water spirits told me all about it. Do you know the Babbling Brook? She knows everything, almost as much as Zeus himself. I hope Zeus doesn't mind my saying that. I mean, he does know everything. Where was I? Oh, yes, being turned into a tree. And not any ordinary tree. . .

Narrator 2: She talked to Hera about everything: the other sprites, the gods, the silly things that mortals did or didn't do.

Narrator 1: Hera tried to be polite at first. Then her neck started getting tired from nodding so much. She found herself wasting valuable time—time when she could have been doing godlike things—just listening to Echo.

Narrator 2: Hera tried talking to Echo.

Hera: Excuse me. . .excuse me. . .Uh, Echo, if I could interrupt. . .EXCUSE ME!

Echo: Oh, my queen, did you want to say something?

Hera: Well, it's about your talking. You know, I hate to say this, but you do go on sometimes.

Echo: Do I? I guess I do. You know, my mother always said the same thing to me. "Echo, my daughter, you do go on," she'd say. But she could talk herself, let me tell you. Once, when I was just a tiny sprite. . .

Hera: (to herself) This is hopeless!

Scene Two: Talk Isn't Cheap

Narrator 1: Hera put up with the long-winded chatter for a long time, but one day her patience ran out.

Hera: Where's my husband? Where's Zeus? There's an emergency about to happen and I can't find him! He'd better not be lazing around. Has anybody seen him?

Echo: I've seen him.

Hera: I was afraid of that.

Narrator 2: Echo had seen her boss, in fact—flirting with some of her fellow sprites! She knew she couldn't let his wife know that. So she kept chattering away with Hera to give time for Zeus to break away.

Echo: He was just here a minute ago. Everybody has to take a break and relax now and again, even if Zeus is supposed to be on duty at all times. Why—

Hera: (getting angrier) Just tell me where—

Echo: I had a cousin who was so serious all the time that he made himself sick. Let me tell you—

Hera: Enough! I can't take it! Silence!

Echo: Why, queen, I didn't know—

Hera: I've got to put a stop to your babbling!

Narrator 1: Hera raised her hand and made this decree.

Hera: From now on, your tireless tongue will rest.
For all of us, even you, this will be best.
For words you have never had a lack,
But now, you have only the power to speak back.

Echo: Speak back.

Hera: That's my royal decree. Do you understand?

Echo: Understand.

Narrator 2: For the rest of time, Echo only had the power to repeat the last words that others said. And that she was bound to do.

Scene Three: Meeting Mr. Wrong

Narrator 1: As you can imagine, Echo felt terrible. All of her feelings were bottled up inside her.

Hera: Now, isn't it wonderful? So peaceful and quiet!

Echo: Quiet!

Narrator 2: When she wasn't serving Hera, Echo began to wander alone in the woods.

Narrator 1: One day, she saw a handsome young man taking a hike. Echo's mood lifted immediately.

Narrator 2: This young man happened to be Narcissus. He was out looking for someone who was good enough to deserve his love.

Narrator 1: When he was a child, his mother had asked a fortune teller if her boy would have a long life. "Perhaps," the prophet had said, "if he never knows himself."

Narcissus: It's a shame that the world is just so full of—how can I put it kindly?—average people. It's just impossible to find anyone who comes near my exacting standards.

Narrator 2: Narcissus had been told by so many people that he was good looking that he was interested mainly in one person: himself!

Narrator 1: But when Echo saw him, she fell hopelessly in love. She followed closely behind him as he wandered in the woods, but she was careful not to reveal herself.

Narrator 2: And, of course, she wanted to say something to this young man, but she had to wait for him to speak first. When Narcissus thought he saw someone moving in a tree's shadow, he called out and Echo got her chance.

Narcissus: Is there someone here?

Echo: Here!

Narcissus: Well, show yourself.

Echo: Show yourself!

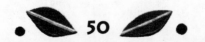

Narcissus: Please come out of hiding. I want to meet you!

Echo: Meet you!

Narcissus: I'm going to leave unless you come out right now!

Echo: Right now!

Narrator 1: As she said those words, she got up her courage and came out from behind the tree where she was hiding. She ran up to Narcissus and tried to hug him.

Narcissus: No, no! Stop! I'm not interested in dating a forest sprite! As a matter of fact, I'd rather die than be in love with you!

Echo: In love with you!

Narcissus: Oh, please. Just leave me alone!

Echo: Alone!

Narrator 2: With that, Narcissus ran away, leaving Echo all alone. She was so upset that she went into a cave to collect her thoughts and have a good cry. That's why they say you can hear Echo's voice even to this day in caves all around the world.

Scene Four: Love at First Sight

Narrator 1: Although Echo had a broken heart, she never lost her love for the handsome Narcissus.

Narrator 2: But a goddess observing the scene didn't feel so kindly toward Narcissus. This was Nemesis, the goddess of "pay-back" forms of justice.

Narrator 1: She's the one who's famous for settling scores.

Nemesis: It's about time that Narcissus had a taste of his own medicine. I'll see to it that he falls in love with someone who always will be outside of his reach!

Narrator 2: So it happened that Narcissus continued his search for someone worthy to be his mate. But he found it to be a very hard search.

Narcissus: It's tiring being perfect, and looking for the perfect companion. I've got to rest and take a drink of water.

Narrator 1: The young man sat down by a beautiful pool and leaned over to take a drink from the clear blue water.

Nemesis: Now, this fellow will get what he deserves.

Narrator 2: As Narcissus bent over he saw his own reflection in the pool.

Narcissus: Hello! Who are you?

Narrator 1: The image just looked back at him without replying.

Narcissus: Why, of all the people I've met in my wanderings, you seem to be the most special. Why won't you tell me your name?

Narrator 2: The reflection just looked back in watery silence.

Narcissus: I feel terrible. Something's coming over me that I've never known before. I feel. . .rejected!

Narrator 1: With that, Narcissus started to feel very, very sorry for himself. A few tears rolled down his cheeks, dropped into the pond—and landed on his reflection. The ripples caused the image to break up and vanish.

Narcissus: No, please, don't go away! Stay, I beg you!

Narrator 2: In a moment, the image returned.

Narcissus: Oh, thank you! I knew you cared about me. You have no idea how many horrible people I had to talk to before I met you.

Narrator 1: Some of the sprites felt badly for Echo. They went to her cave to cheer her up. They told Echo about the odd young man who had fallen in love with his own image. She went out to laugh at this pitiful creature—but then realized it was Narcissus!

Narrator 2: She felt pity for Narcissus and decided to watch over him. Her voice repeated his words.

Narcissus: (speaking to his reflection) I promise I'll never leave you!

Echo: Never leave you.

Narrator 1: Narcissus was so absorbed in his own conversation that he didn't hear Echo at all.

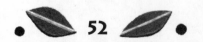

Narcissus: I'll never move from this spot.

Echo: From this spot.

Narrator 2: And that's just how Narcissus spent the rest of his short life, sitting by the pond, in love with his own reflection.

Narrator 1: In the spot where the young man spent his last days, there grew a beautiful flower in springtime. It was the flower that now bears his name: the narcissus. And Echo? Listen hard, and you may be able to hear her talking if someone speaks loudly enough.

The End

FOR THE TEACHER

Talk About It

- There's no doubt that Echo is a chatterbox. But is she completely at fault when Hera gives her that big punishment? Why is Zeus partly to blame?

- What kind of a person is Narcissus? Make a list of words to describe him. Explain why he's "narcissistic"—the word we get from his own name meaning totally in love with himself—instead of someone who simply has a healthy self-image.

- Why is the punishment that the goddess Nemesis puts on Narcissus especially fitting for his personality? If Nemesis—the goddess of settling scores—was acting in the world today, what kinds of criminals would you want her to go after? What kinds of punishments could she make up to fit the crimes?

Extension Activities

- **Write a Poem** Teach students about the power of repetition by having them write an echo poem. Ask students to construct a twenty-line unrhymed poem, with every other line being a repetition of the last three words of the previous line. Ask students to discuss how repetition affects the meaning of the poem. You may want to read a poem such as Dylan Thomas' "Do Not Go Gentle Into That Good Night" as you prepare students for this exercise.

- **Self Portraits** Challenge students to imagine that they're staring at themselves, like Narcissus, in a pool of water. What do they see? Challenge them to draw portraits of themselves at their best (best hair, smile, outfit, etc.). In addition, their portraits should somehow include what students think are some of their best inner qualities (generosity, ability to do math, etc.). Students might want to write those qualities somewhere on the portrait, or draw symbols of the qualities.

- **Legacy** Challenge student groups to create an advertising campaign that stresses the message: "Don't Be Like Narcissus." Students may want to cut out pictures that show self-absorbed people acting in particularly grating ways, or celebrities/models demonstrating what it means to be self-absorbed. Others may wish to write a brief guide or rules book that outlines what is and isn't narcissistic behavior. Encourage groups to include drawings or pictures of the narcissus flower in their design.

LEGENDS OF THE FALL:

THE STORY OF ODYSSEUS, HELEN AND THE CITY OF TROY

In this myth a warrior named Odysseus scrambles to find a way to end a long war that has been raging between his Greek army and the city of Troy. His bold gamble, using a big wooden horse, looks like it has a chance of working. But will the smart and beautiful Helen see through his tricks and destroy the Greeks' hope of success?

Characters (in order of appearance)

Poet, narrator
Muse, goddess of poetry; another narrator
Odysseus (oh-DIS-ee-us), a Greek commander and king
Sinon (SIGH-non), Greek soldier
People

Priam (PRI-am), king of Troy
Trojan Soldier
Laocoön (lay-AWK-uh-wahn), the high priest of Poseidon
Helen, a captive who was taken to Troy
Greek Soldier

Words to Watch For
Epeos (eh-PAY-us), Greek carpenter
Troy (TROI), city in present-day Turkey, east of Greece

Aeneus (ih-NEE-us), Trojan soldier
Athena, goddess of wisdom

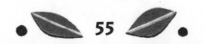

Introduction

Poet: Sing through me, Muse—goddess of poetry—and let me tell everyone the epic story of the battle between the Greeks and the people of Troy.

Muse: I'll do better than that. I'll help you tell the story myself.

Poet: It's a deal. Where shall we start?

Muse: Let's start near the end. After ten bloody years of fighting, the Greeks still hadn't captured the faraway city of Troy. They had been fighting Troy to win back Helen, said to be the world's most beautiful woman, who had been taken away from her Greek husband by a Trojan prince.

Poet: The Greeks had lost some of their best fighters in battle, including a great warrior named Achilles. After ten years, they still hadn't gotten much further than where they first landed on the beach. They were tired, homesick and ready to give up.

Muse: That's right. Only Commander Odysseus, the most clever of the Greeks, wasn't willing to quit. He just kept planning and plotting.

Scene One: In the Greek Camp

Odysseus: (holding his head in his hands) There must be something we haven't tried. We've attacked and attacked, but we've never made headway.

Sinon: (joking) What we need is for someone on the inside to open the city gates and just let us in. Ha! Imagine that! Walking right into Troy? Now that would be something!

Odysseus: But that's it! We'll get inside and open the gates!

Sinon: Are you crazy? Haven't we been trying to do that for ten years? Nothing has worked, remember? Let's go home while we still can.

Odysseus: But what if we somehow got a handful of soldiers into the city? Say they were in a. . .box. They could sneak out at night and open the gates. We'd conquer the city in ten minutes!

Sinon: Yeah, right, and if I were Athena I'd fly. How are you going to get a box full of soldiers past the Trojan guards?

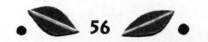

Odysseus: I've got an idea. We'll get a huge wooden horse, as big as a great statue, but keep it hollow so that twenty soldiers can fit inside. The Trojans won't know that it is hollow, so they'll never look inside.

Sinon: And I suppose you just happen to have one of these giant horses?

Odysseus: No, but Epeos our carpenter could make one. If he can make a ship, he can certainly make this horse. Athena can inspire him if he needs help.

Sinon: All right, then what?

Odysseus: We leave this gigantic horse right here on the beach. They think it's an offering we made to the gods. That will make them open up their gates and pull it right inside. A little trick will do what ten years of fighting never could.

Sinon: But where will our armies be?

Odysseus: We'll pack up our ships and leave—only we won't really leave. We'll just sail out of sight and wait until the horse gets taken inside Troy. Our soldiers will unlock the gates, give us the signal and we'll march right in.

Sinon: Okay, but the Trojans aren't dumb. After ten years of fighting us, aren't they going to be mighty suspicious?

Odysseus: Well. . .That's where you'd come in.

Sinon: Me?

Scene Two: Inside Troy

Muse: Weeks later, the Trojans awoke to a very strange sound. Silence.

Poet: The Trojan lookouts climbed to their posts on top of the walled city to see what was happening in the Greek camp. They were shocked! The Greek soldiers had disappeared. The ground was covered with empty tents, broken weapons, and other gear that the Greeks had left behind. Above all this garbage stood a huge horse.

Muse: The horse was wooden and almost as tall as the gates of Troy. It stood proudly and silently, as if it wanted to challenge the Trojans one more time.

Poet: When the Trojan people heard that the Greeks had gone, they started celebrating.

People: The war is over! We've won, after all these years! Three cheers for the boys in bronze!

Poet: But Troy's King Priam and his royal fortune-teller, Laocoön, told the people not to celebrate too soon.

Priam: Let's make sure this isn't just a trick. Laocoön, you and I and a party of warriors will go down and see if the Greeks have really gone.

Poet: The Trojans walked down to the shore where the Greeks had made their camp. Everywhere the Trojans found memories of the fierce battles that had been fought and the heroes who had taken up arms.

Priam: Look, this was the tent that Odysseus stayed in. And over there, that was Achilles' camp.

Muse: But what everyone wanted to see was the giant wooden horse.

Priam: What could it be? Why would the Greeks build it only to leave it behind?

Laocoön: Whatever it is, I don't like it. I've never trusted the Greeks and I'm not going to start now. Let's burn this thing to the ground right now. It'll make a great bonfire!

Poet: Following the fortune-teller's orders, soldiers collected wood and piled it under the horse. Laocoön was just about to throw a torch on the pile and start the blaze when a group of Trojan soldiers appeared.

Trojan Soldier: Wait, we've just arrested a prisoner!

Muse: They brought out Sinon, Odysseus' comrade. His hands were bound in front of him and he was dressed in rags.

Priam: Who are you and where are the rest of your men? Tell us soon or you'll feel the points of our swords.

Sinon: There's no need to threaten me. I'll gladly tell you everything you want to know about my rotten countrymen. (to himself) I hope I get this right or Odysseus will kill me.

Priam: Are you a traitor?

Sinon: No, I'm a survivor. Thank goodness you found me! The Greeks' fortune-tellers told them that they would never win the war because Athena, the goddess of wisdom, was mad at them. The best thing to do, they said, was to make a human sacrifice to Athena and then go home. I was chosen to be the sacrifice—but I escaped!

Laocoön: A likely story! What about this big horse?

Sinon: It was meant to be a gift for Athena, too.

Priam: Why did they make it so big?

Sinon: So you wouldn't be able to move it into your city. They didn't want you to get the credit and good luck from Athena.

Priam: Ha! We'll show them. We'll move this horse right into the center of our city, next to Athena's temple.

Laocoön: No, your highness, don't do it! Something smells bad here. I don't trust Greeks, even when they bring gifts. Let's destroy the horse and kill the prisoner.

Poet: Just then a strange and horrible thing happened. Two huge snakes reared out of the ocean surf and raced toward the men standing on the beach. Before Laocoön could say another word, the serpents wrapped themselves around him. As the other Trojans looked on in horror, the serpents squeezed him to death, then slithered off toward Athena's temple in the city.

Priam: Athena must have sent those snakes as a sign! Let's hear no more doubts. Take this horse into the city!

Muse: But Priam was wrong. Athena hadn't sent those serpents. Poseidon, the sea god who loved the Greeks, had sent the snakes to help Odysseus' plot!

Scene Three: Inside Troy

Poet: With great effort, the Trojans dragged the horse into the city. Priam declared a city-wide celebration. He opened the special storehouses that were locked up during the war. All Trojans, young and old, ate and drank their fill for the first time in years.

Muse: Inside the horse, Odysseus and the other Greek soldiers heard the Trojans singing and dancing, and waited for their chance.

Poet: Hours later, as the party was ending, Priam brought Helen to the horse.

Muse: Remember that the whole Trojan war had started over Helen, who had been taken away from her home in Greece and kept in Troy. While she was in Troy, she became very friendly with the Trojans. Sometimes it was difficult to say whose side she was on.

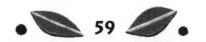

Priam: Helen, you're like a daughter to me. You must help me. What do you think of this horse? Do you think it could be some kind of Greek trick?

Helen: (whispering) Priam, if this is a trick, only the mind of Odysseus could have thought of it. Only he would think to, say, hide some soldiers inside!

Priam: (whispering back, alarmed) Do you think there are soldier inside??

Helen: (whispering again) I have a test that will tell us for sure. I know the Greeks. I'll speak as if I'm their wives. If they have hearts, they won't be able to resist saying something back!

Poet: Helen circled the big horse three times, patting it and calling out in the voices of the wives the Greeks hadn't seen in ten years. Inside the horse, the soldiers had to bite their hands and stuff their mouths full of cloth to keep from crying out.

Helen: This is not a trick, Priam. Go on with the celebrations!

Poet: When the city had partied itself to exhaustion and sleep, everything became quiet. Then, there was the sound of a trap door being opened and the scuffling of feet. In a moment the Greek warriors stood inside the city.

Odysseus: (whispering) Four of you go and unlock the gates. The rest of you find where the Trojans keep their weapons. Set as many fires as you can. The flames will signal our ships that it's time to return.

Muse: The Greeks carried out their chores in deadly silence. By the time the Trojans awoke to the smell of smoke, it was already too late.

Trojan Soldier: The city is in chaos—those Greeks must be the cause of this!

Greek Soldier: (striking the Trojan with his sword) Right you are!

Poet: Greek soldiers held the groggy Trojans at bay until the gates burst open and what seemed like a flood of Greeks charged into Priam's city.

Muse: What followed was not pretty, but then war is always ugly. Many people—children, women and men alike—died at the hands of the victorious Greeks. Those who survived were forced into slavery. The great city of Troy, which had stood for so many years, was completely burned to the ground.

Poet: But there was one bright spot in all this horror. One Trojan soldier named Aeneas managed to survive the destruction, along with his family. It was he who sailed away and,

legend has it, started a new city in the distant land of Italy. That city would one day be called Rome. As for Helen, she returned to Greece where she was reunited with her husband.

The End

FOR THE TEACHER

Talk About It

- It is said that Helen's beauty "launched a thousand ships" and began the Trojan War in the first place. Is beauty that powerful in our society today? How and how not? Why are wars started and fought these days?

- How does Odysseus use his wits to plan a turning point in the war? Could his plans have succeeded without help from the gods? Why or why not?

- There are different versions of what Helen's role was in this story. Some say she was kidnapped from Greece and taken to Troy against her will, while others say she left Greece willingly, under the influence of a god's spell. Likewise, some versions say she knew Odysseus was entering Troy in disguise but refused to give him away, while the version upon which this play is based says she did her best to help the Trojan side when the horse was brought into Troy. Most versions agree that Helen returned to Greece after the war ended and was reunited with her husband there. Given all these conflicting points of view, what can be said for sure about Helen? What questions would you want to ask if you could interview her?

Extension Activities

- **Crossfire** Challenge groups of students to imagine that they are in Troy covering the end of the war for a newspaper. Their first task is to brainstorm a list of topics they could write about. (Possibilities would include: descriptions of morale in Troy and in Odysseus' camp before the final showdown; an interview with Helen about what would be the best way to end the conflict; interviews with Trojan citizens regarding their opinions of Helen and the price her presence has cost the city; coverage of the final battle strategy, with diagrams showing how it was played out; descriptions of the final battle carnage; opposing editorials regarding the fairness of Odysseus' Trojan-horse strategy.) Next, groups should divide up chosen topics among group members. Lastly, encourage groups to include maps in their spreads that show the approximate locations of Troy and Sparta (where Helen came from).

- **Having Her Say** Expand on the last set of questions in the previous section and challenge students to rewrite this myth from Helen's point of view. Students may wish to read other versions of this myth, to flesh out their stories. What does Helen think of Paris, the Trojan prince who kidnaps her from her Greek husband? What does she think of the ten-year war that is waged on the Trojan people to get her back? What is it like to live in a strange new place and think you're never going to see your family

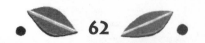

again? Encourage students to address these and other questions in their renderings. After volunteers have read their work, lead a discussion about the roles of women in ancient Greek society, based on what students have read in these plays. Just what is a woman's "place" in Greek life? A man's "place"?

- **Legacy** Trickery during wartime hardly ended with the Trojan-horse affair. Encourage students to conduct an investigation of techniques the United States has used to trick some of its enemies during war. Male and female spies served their country during the Revolutionary, Civil and World Wars—and the army went to great lengths to trick the Germans into believing that D-Day would take place at a different spot along the French coast, using everything from fake messages to inflatable jeeps and tanks. Challenge groups to research and retell some of these stories.

SEA TREK:

THE STORY OF ODYSSEUS AND HIS TRAVELS

In this myth the Greek warrior Odysseus and a boatload of soldiers set out to sail home after their long years of fighting in distant Troy. Along the way they make several unplanned pit-stops—at islands with one-eyed giants who enjoy human snacks, for example. It will take wits, wisdom and more than a little help from some god-friends to pull off this "Odyssey."

Characters (in order of appearance)

Athena (uh-THEE-nuh), goddess of wisdom; narrator
Homer, a storyteller; narrator
Crew Member 1
Crew Member 2
Odysseus, Greek commander and king
Crew Member 3

Circe (SIR-see), a crafty witch
Hermes (HER-meez), messenger god
Cyclops (SIGH-clops), a one-eyed monster
Neighbors, monsters who live near the Cyclops

Words to Watch For
Ismaros (is-MAR-us), legendary Mediterranean island
Ithaca (ITH-ih-kuh), Greek island

Introduction

Athena: Long ago a soldier named Odysseus helped the Greeks defeat their enemies the Trojans in a long and bloody war.

Homer: During the days of celebrating that followed, though, the Greeks completely forgot to thank their gods for bringing them victory.

Athena: And, believe me, we gods get angry when you humans don't say thank you! To punish the Greeks, the gods sent confusing winds that blew the Greeks' ships off-course as they made their long voyages home.

Homer: Some Greeks had to wrestle with gods before they were allowed home. Others simply met a watery fate.

Athena: Even Odysseus, whose clever ways I have always loved, was given a hard time. Though I helped the man whenever I could, he had to fight his own battles to get home to his wife and his son.

Homer: I composed an epic story called the *Odyssey* about Odysseus' struggle to get home again. It's a big story, but with the help of Athena, I'll tell you a bit of it!

Scene One: Learning to Retreat

Homer: After leaving the wrecked city of Troy, Odysseus and his crew set sail for Greece. But the gods' ill-winds drove them first to the island of Ismaros, whose residents were fierce fighters who hated strangers.

Crew Member 1: Captain, I see land and a city!

Crew Member 2: We're starving. We haven't eaten since we left Troy. And we've run out of wine! We've got to go ashore.

Odysseus: No, let's try to keep heading for home.

Crew Member 1: Captain, if you tell us no, don't be surprised if we mutiny and go there anyway. Then, you'll have to row home by yourself.

Crew Member 2: Yeah, what are you afraid of? If we can beat the Trojans we can handle anything that comes our way.

Odysseus: All right, we'll go ashore, but make it quick!

Homer: When the Greeks landed they defeated the island's warriors right on the beach, though one or two of the island soldiers escaped and ran into the thick forest nearby. Then they began to feast on the goats and wine they found at hand.

Crew Member 1: Hey, this wine's strong! One sip practically knocked me off my feet! Too bad there's only a few gallons for each of us, ha ha! (to Odysseus) Captain, why aren't you drinking and celebrating?

Odysseus: (looking off into the hills) This is no time for a party. Those warriors who got away could have gone for help. We could be attacked at any moment.

Athena: Odysseus was right. An army of warriors had already surrounded the feasting soldiers. With a shout, they attacked.

Homer: The Greeks were caught off guard, but Odysseus organized a brilliant retreat. He and his men made it back to their ship, though many lives were lost.

Athena: As the Greeks mourned their dead comrades, Odysseus warned the crew.

Odysseus: We lost more soldiers just now on Ismaros than we did in Troy! We can't afford to be careless. (to himself) I hope I can keep them in line until we get home!

Scene Two: Bewitched!

Homer: For nine days the sea and wind became mysteriously calm.

Athena: The men rowed, but they seemed to get nowhere. Supplies were again running low.

Homer: But then a powerful current brought them to an island that looked peaceful.

Crew Member 1: What can happen to us there, Captain? We've got to go ashore for more water or we'll die of thirst!

Odysseus: Listen to me. This time we're going to send a search party to explore the island first. They can tell us if it's safe. (pointing to Crew Members 2 and 3) You two, go with him and see if the islanders here are peaceful. Be back before sunset.

Crew Members 1, 2 and 3: Aye, aye, captain!

Homer: When the soldiers went inland, they found themselves lost in a deep forest. Suddenly, they stumbled into a clearing.

Athena: Before them they saw a cave, covered with vines. Outside the cave burned a fire of sweet-smelling wood. They saw a beautiful woman weaving and singing.

Homer: But the strangest thing of all was that around the cave lay wild animals—lions and wolves—that acted just like house cats and puppy dogs. The woman called to the men.

Circe: Welcome, you weary travelers! I can see you've had a hard voyage. My home is your home.

Athena: She led the men to beautiful thrones inside the cave and sat them before a table covered with jugs of wine, wheels of cheese, barley-cakes and honey. The half-starved men feasted and feasted.

Circe: Are you comfortable now?

Crew Member 1: Oh, yes! I'm afraid we've made pigs of ourselves.

Circe: What an interesting choice of words!

Homer: At that moment Circe raised a magic wand and uttered a strange spell. In a flash, the men lost their human features and began growing snouts and tails. They had been turned into pigs! Circe herded them into a pig pen, where they squealed in vain for help.

Athena: Only one of the Greek scouts remained in human form. He hadn't liked what he saw when they arrived at the cave, and had hidden himself in nearby trees to see what would happen. Shocked by what he saw, he now ran back to the ship to tell Odysseus about the disaster.

Odysseus: I need the gods' help now!

Homer: In answer to that prayer, the messenger-god Hermes brought down a word of advice from Mount Olympus.

Hermes: Take this plant and eat it. It will protect you from the witch's charms. But you must face her yourself if you want to free your companions.

Athena: So Odysseus started the difficult hike through the island forest, clutching his special gift from Hermes all the while. At last, he reached the witch's cave. It was hard to miss, with its big pen of squealing and grunting pigs.

Odysseus: (to Circe) I'm looking for a group of men that passed through this area this morning. Have you seen them?

Circe: (charmingly) I don't believe so. But have some food and something to drink and maybe I'll remember.

Homer: Circe took Odysseus in to the same table that was set with yet another feast. When he had eaten and drunk, the witch smiled and raised her wand.

Circe: Now, into the pen with you. You'll be the head pig!

Athena: But Odysseus, still a man, pulled out his sword and shouted.

Odysseus: No more tricks! You see, the gods are on my side. Now turn my men back to the way they were, and be quick about it!

Homer: And so she did. Not long afterwards, Odysseus and his men shoved off from the frightening island and set sail for home once again.

Scene Three: The Captain's Curiosity

Athena: The ship sailed on for a day or two, but then a thick fog covered the Great Sea. The crew members couldn't see each other, let alone where they were going. Their luck seemed to be going from bad to worse.

Homer: Just when a little gust of wind blew a tiny window in the fog, a lookout shouted that the ship was about to run aground! The men stopped rowing. A few feet ahead of them was a beautiful green island. High above them, on some kind of cliff, they could hear a waterfall. Here and there they spotted goats and other animals.

Crew Member 2: How beautiful! The gods must have brought us here to make up for our bad luck in the past.

Athena: Everyone agreed. The gods were finally on their side again. Or so they thought. Carefully, the crew got out and hunted some wild goats. They cooked up a meal and were pleased to be left in peace.

Odysseus: Before we leave, I'd like to know who lives on this island. I'll take some men with me and do a little exploring.

Homer: This time Odysseus' curiosity got the better of him. Before setting out, though, something told him that he should pack a few jugs of the strong wine he had gotten on Ismaros. It was advice he would later thank the gods for.

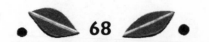

Athena: Odysseus and his men discovered a huge cave. A boulder lay next to the entrance. Inside the cave were pens where goats and sheep were kept. Whoever lived there made cheese from the animals' milk.

Crew Member 1: Captain, haven't we seen enough? Why don't we take some goats and some cheese for our journey? We can leave the wine as payment and be on our way.

Odysseus: Not so fast! Look at that huge fire! Look at that chair! Whoever lives in this cave must be a giant! I've never seen a giant. Let's stay and get a look at him so we'll have some good stories to tell the kids when we get home.

Scene Four: Uninvited Guests

Homer: As they were speaking, they heard the rumble of footsteps. Quickly, they ran to the back of the cave.

Odysseus: (whispering to his crew) Now don't be rude. From the looks of this cave, whoever lives here must be quite civilized.

Athena: First, a herd of sheep—big creatures, almost as large as cows, with heavy woolen coats—raced into the cave. Then a gigantic body stepped into the entrance of the cave, blocking out the light. The Greeks heard the scraping sound of the boulder being rolled across the opening.

Homer: They saw sparks that told them someone was starting a fire. As the flames grew, they could finally see who lived in the cave

Odysseus: (whispering) Look how hideous!

Crew Member 1: (hissing) Let's get out of here now.

Crew Member 2: We can't! We're trapped!

Athena: The giant was massive, with arms and legs the size of oak trees. He had only one eye, right in the center of his forehead.

Homer: The men tried to remain hidden in the back of the cave, but as luck would have it, one of the Greeks who was surrounded by goats sneezed. The Cyclops—for that was the name the Greeks gave such beings—looked up.

Cyclops: Who's there? Show yourselves! Tell me what you're doing here!

Athena: Then Odysseus, who had gotten his men into this mess, spoke up.

Odysseus: We're trying to find our way home but fate brought us to this island. We are friendly travelers. Don't forget that it's good luck to be nice to travelers.

Cyclops: Big deal. Why do I have to worry about what the gods like or don't like? Tell me, are there more of you on the island?

Homer: Always quick on his feet, Odysseus made up a story.

Odysseus: No, just us! Our ship crashed against the rocks and we were the only ones who survived.

Cyclops: Well, in that case, you'll make several small, but tasty meals. I get so tired of goat cheese and leg of lamb!

Homer: Suddenly, the Cyclops grabbed two of Odysseus' crew members. The sound of screams pierced the cave. Odysseus and the rest of his men were horrified.

Odysseus: You can't just murder us! The gods, who protect all strangers, will punish you!

Cyclops: Ha! I'm protected by Poseidon. The sea god is my father! No one can punish me.

Athena: The next morning, the Cyclops grabbed two more of Odysseus' men and ate them for breakfast. Then, he moved aside the rock to let his sheep out to graze.

Homer: As he left the cave the giant rolled the stone back to trap the Greeks inside.

Cyclops: I'll see you for dinner, ha ha!

Scene Five: A Plan

Odysseus: We can't just sit here and wait. But we can't kill the Cyclops. He's the only one strong enough to move the rock away. If he dies, we'll be trapped in this cave. Wait. . .I've got a plan.

Athena: When the Cyclops returned to the cave that night, Odysseus was ready for him.

Odysseus: Oh, great sir! We're very sorry we've trespassed on your property. Please accept a gift from us.

Cyclops: A gift? For me? You shouldn't have. What is it?

Odysseus: Some delicious wine! Please accept it and be merciful to us.

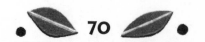

Homer: Now this Ismaros wine was very strong stuff. People always added twenty gallons of water to each jug because a cup of the pure wine would knock them off their feet. Odysseus, though, offered the whole jug of pure wine to the Cyclops—and he downed the whole thing in one gulp!

Cyclops: Thank you, er—What did you say your name was?

Odysseus: I'm called No One. I'm the son of Nobody.

Cyclops: Strange names you people have. Well, No One, I will be merciful. I'll eat you last, how's that!

Homer: Then, sleepy from the wine, the Cyclops stretched out on the floor of the cave. Soon he was snoring so loudly that the Greeks thought their eardrums would burst.

Athena: Odysseus and his comrades took a long pole from one of the sheep pens. They sharpened it and put it into the fire until it glowed.

Homer: Then, with Odysseus leading the charge, they rammed the pole with all their strength, aiming it at the Cyclops' only eye.

Athena: The Cyclops roared out in pain. His cries woke up other Cyclops people who lived nearby. They stood outside his blocked-up cave and called in.

Neighbors: What's happened to you? Are you OK?

Cyclops: No One has hurt me! No One has blinded me!

Neighbors: Well, if no one has bothered you, don't disturb us.

Homer: Now the Cyclops was determined to eat every last one of the Greeks.

Cyclops: It will take me longer to find you, but you can't escape. I'll keep you holed up in this pen until I've found each and every one of you!

Athena: When the Cyclops let out his big sheep the next day, Odysseus whispered to his men that this was their chance to escape.

Odysseus: Each of you hold onto the bottom of one of the sheep. Let them carry you out! But don't let the Cyclops touch you, or we'll all be dead men!

Homer: The men did as their leader ordered. They slung themselves under the ox-sized sheep and grabbed hold of the thick wool, making sure to stay out of the reach of the Cyclops.

Athena: The Cyclops touched each sheep before he let it out of the cave to make sure he wasn't letting any of the humans escape. But he only patted the sheep's back, never suspecting that the men could be riding underneath.

Cyclops: There, there, my pretty lambs. You can see the light of day, while those men will rot in darkness. That is, until I find them.

Homer: Odysseus was the last to leave the cave. He didn't know that he had hitched a ride under one of the Cyclops' favorite sheep. The giant patted the old ram on the back and spoke to it.

Cyclops: Oh, my pet, I may be blind, but I know you! But why are you so slow today? You're usually the first one out to the pasture. You must be upset about my eye. Don't worry, I'll make No One pay for this!

Athena: The monster's hand came within an inch of Odysseus, but that wasn't close enough! The old ram ran out of the cave and Odysseus was free.

Homer: When the Greeks were all safely aboard their boat, Odysseus couldn't resist taunting the Cyclops.

Odysseus: (shouting to the Cyclops) Hey Cyclops, aren't you looking for us? Sorry we couldn't stay for another meal!

Cyclops: (emerging from his cave) How did you miserable little rats get out? Well, here's a parting gift for you!

Athena: Aiming in the direction of the voice, the Cyclops hurled a huge stone that just missed sinking Odysseus' ship.

Crew Member 1: Shhh! Captain, please, you'll get us all killed.

Odysseus: I can't help myself. (shouting to Cyclops) In case anyone asks who's outsmarted you, tell them Odysseus from Ithaca was the man!

Cyclops: Odysseus! So that's your real name! I've heard it before! May Poseidon, my father, make your travels hard to bear! If fate says you must reach home, so be it. But let your journey be filled with torment!

Homer: Poseidon the sea god listened to his son's request. He sent storms, monsters and shipwrecks Odysseus' way. The hero lost his ship and his crew. If the goddess Athena hadn't stepped in to save his life several times, Odysseus too would have died. But he made it home. He defeated even more enemies when he returned to his kingdom in Ithaca and regained his throne.

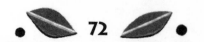

Athena: I admit Odysseus is my favorite human. He's very smart—and I am the goddess of wisdom, after all!

Homer: Even today we remember Odysseus' bold spirit when we call a difficult journey an odyssey.

The End

FOR THE TEACHER

Talk About It

- What makes Odysseus a good leader? What weaknesses take away from his strengths?

- How do the gods affect what happens on this journey home? How do choices made by the humans make things worse? Could Odysseus and his men have survived without the gods stepping in? Why or why not?

- According to this myth, there were all kinds of monsters and strange beings living in the Mediterranean area—yet we certainly don't know of any Cyclops or Circe-like creatures living in that area today. Do you think the Greek audiences really believed and feared that these creatures existed, or were they just having fun? Could you say these myths might have been popular then for the same kinds of reasons that shows like the "X-Files" are popular today? Why or why not?

Extension Activities

- **Odysseus Is Us** Odysseus and his crew go through some wild experiences. What would this story be like if Odysseus were a middle-school student living today? What kinds of challenges would he face instead of one-eyed giants and animal-loving witches? What would his goals be? Ask your students to think about a "modernized" *Odyssey* in which the main character is a student their age (girl or boy). Break your class up into groups and ask each group to come up with a plot outline for their "revised" classic.

- **Courage Under Fire?** Was Odysseus a good leader? Stage a debate in your class about his leadership skills. Divide the class evenly and ask one side to be critical of Odysseus and the other side to defend the hero. Using examples from this play, decide whether Odysseus should be praised for his actions or court-martialed.

- **Legacy** A good number of popular books and movies are at least indirectly influenced in their form by the story of Odysseus and his travels. Challenge groups of students to name books, shows or movies that they believe have been influenced by this story. Encourage them to describe the similarities and differences between their choices and the *Odyssey*.

SPEED:

THE STORY OF ATALANTA

In this myth the men who fall in love with a beautiful young woman named Atalanta must race her for her heart. It's no easy task, as Atalanta just happens to be the best runner and hunter in the Greek world—and the price of defeat in a race with her is death.

Characters (in order of appearance)

Girl, narrator
Artemis (ART-uh-mis), goddess of hunting; another narrator
Father, Atalanta's father
Oeneus (EE-nee-us), king and the father of Meleager
Althaea (al-THEE-uh), queen and the mother of Meleager
Meleager (mel-ee-AY-guhr), prince
Atalanta (at-uh-LANT-uh), hunter and athlete

Uncle 1, uncle of Meleager
Uncle 2, uncle of Meleager
Servant 1
Fates, the weavers of life
Servant 2
Suitor 1
Suitor 2
Hippomenes (hip-AHM-uh-neez), admirer of Atalanta

Introduction

Girl: (thinking out loud) All these Greek stories are about men doing amazing things. Why aren't there any myths about women heroes?

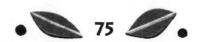

Artemis: (appearing suddenly) Well, what about the story of Atalanta, one of the greatest hunters and athletes that ever lived?

Girl: (surprised) Who on earth are you and where did you come from?

Artemis: I'm Artemis, the goddess of hunting. And be more polite to me in the future, my dear. I've turned people into trees for not minding their manners.

Girl: Yes, your goddess. . .I mean, your huntress. . .I mean. . .

Artemis: Don't worry about titles. Just listen to the story.

Scene One: Atalanta Meets Meleager

Artemis: When Atalanta was born, her father the king was sad, not happy, like many Greek fathers of his day.

Father: I wanted a boy who would become a great hunter and make me proud. There's nothing I can do with this girl—take her away and just leave her on a mountainside somewhere!

Girl: What a rat her father was!

Artemis: He was a rat, but he wasn't a successful rat. The baby girl lived!

Girl: But how?

Artemis: Animals proved kinder than humans. A family of bears adopted the child and raised her as their own. They taught her the secrets of the forest. She became a great hunter. With amazing speed she could chase down her prey. And with her sharp eyes and steady hands, she became a deadly shot with her bow and arrow.

Girl: But if she stayed all by herself in the woods, how did she become famous?

Artemis: I'm afraid I had something to do with that. One day I got rather mad at one of the local rulers, King Oeneus, for not paying enough attention to my temples. They were getting a bit run-down, you see, and people weren't making offerings to me anymore. I sent the good king a little present. Actually, it was quite a big present.

Girl: I bet he was pleased.

Artemis: Would you be pleased if a giant, fire-breathing boar with razor-sharp tusks appeared in your backyard?

Oeneus: (shouting) A boar! Help me! Help my kingdom! Oh, somebody do something!

Althaea: What's so special about this wild pig? Send someone out to kill it and we'll put an apple in its mouth and have it for supper.

Oeneus: (trembling) I'm afraid that won't do, my dear. This boar is as big as an ox. Its tusks can slice down trees. Flames shoot out from its snout! And it's destroying all our crops. If we don't stop it soon, we'll have no harvest!

Althaea: Well, then send all the best hunters in the world after it. Together they can bring it down, I'm sure.

Artemis: So a call went out for help from Greece's greatest hunters. Some of the top shots who showed up included a brave warrior named Jason and Theseus of Athens. Oeneus' son, Meleager, and his two uncles headed the hunting party.

Meleager: What a group of heroes! This will go down in history as one of the greatest hunts of all time. Wait a minute. Who's that?

Artemis: Atalanta strolled into the middle of the crowd. Her beautiful hair was knotted in a pony tail. She had an ivory quiver full of arrows slung over her shoulder and a powerful bow in her hand.

Atalanta: I've heard you need someone who's a good shot.

Artemis: At that very second. Meleager fell in love with Atalanta. Unfortunately, not everyone was so thrilled to have Atalanta on the hunt.

Uncle 1: A woman on a hunt! Who ever heard of anything so foolish! She'll be nothing but trouble, I know it. Send her away!

Meleager: No, she stays. I'll bet she proves to be the best hunter of us all!

Uncle 2: (grumbling to Uncle 1) She's already bewitched our nephew. We'll have to keep an eye on her.

Scene Two: The Hunt

Artemis: Remembering their purpose, the hunters put aside their disagreements over Atalanta and set out to defeat the gigantic boar.

Uncle 1: We'll search high and low for that overgrown pig.

Uncle 2: I don't see that ugly beast anywhere. Let's look deeper in the woods.

Artemis: So they stepped carefully into the darkest part of the forest. In the midst of the tall trees and fallen branches, the hunters grew nervous.

Uncle 1: (in a scared voice) Look out! Oh, sorry. I thought that stump over there was the—

Meleager: There it is!

Artemis: My big boar had seen the hunters before they saw it. It raced right past them, leaving them in great confusion. Their weapons went flying in all different directions. Only luck had kept the hunters from killing each other.

Meleager: Hey, next time look where you're throwing that spear!

Uncle 1: I didn't throw that one! My spear landed over in that tree. Oh, no! Here comes the boar again!

Artemis: Only Atalanta kept her cool. As the boar crashed through the trees she aimed one of her arrows carefully and let it fly. The missile struck the boar right behind the ear and knocked it down.

Atalanta: Now, Meleager, use your spear and finish the job!

Meleager: I'll try. . .

Artemis: With that, the prince thrust his spear into the unlucky boar, killing it and freeing the people from its deadly rampages.

Meleager: Atalanta, you drew the first blood from this beast. You deserve to have these trophies—the tusks and the hide.

Uncle 1: (angrily) Wait a minute, nephew. You killed the beast! The prizes are yours, not that she-bear's!

Meleager: Please watch your tongue, Uncle. Atalanta deserves the prize, just as she deserves my love.

Atalanta: Prince, I don't know what to say. . .

Uncle 2: I do! You're not getting any prize and you're certainly not getting my nephew! You're just a nobody from the wrong side of the forest.

Artemis: With that, the uncles turned their weapons toward Atalanta. Meleager was prepared. In love and in a rage, he drew his sword and killed them both!

Scene Three: Althaea's Revenge

Artemis: When Queen Althaea, Meleager's mother, heard what happened at the hunt, she was torn apart inside.

Althaea: How could my son have done such a terrible thing? He killed his own uncles to defend that wild girl. My brothers must be avenged. But to avenge them would mean that I'd have to kill my own son! What can I do?

Artemis: After hours of agonizing thought, she decided that there was no other choice. Her own son would have to give up his life to pay for the deaths of his uncles.

Althaea: Servant! Go to the back of my closet and tap on the wall. When you hear a hollow sound, you will have found my secret hiding place. Break down the wall and bring me the chest that I've kept hidden there all these years.

Artemis: The servant did as the queen commanded. In time she returned with a wooden box that was covered with twenty years' worth of dust. Althaea opened the box and took out an old log that had been charred by a fire.

Althaea: Put this on the fire!

Artemis: The servant thought it strange, but did as the queen commanded. She returned to find the queen sobbing.

Servant 1: I've carried out your orders, great Queen. But can you tell me why you kept that plain old log for so many years?

Althaea: It's a story that pains me. One night when Meleager was just a baby, I sat before the fire, singing my child to sleep. I must have fallen asleep, too, because I had a terrible dream.

Servant 1: What was it, your highness?

Althaea: I dreamed I saw the Three Fates—the old women who weave the events of our lives and decide when we will die—holding a short piece of yarn.

Fates: The boy's life will not be long! It will end when the log in that fireplace burns out!

Althaea: I leapt up and, with my bare hands, pulled the burning log from the fireplace. I put out the flames and hid the log so that no harm could come to my son. But now, my son has killed my brothers. . .(starts to cry)

Artemis: The servant turned to look at the log blazing away in the fireplace. Meanwhile, in the forest, Meleager and Atalanta were talking.

Meleager: Atalanta, you're brave, strong and beautiful. (gasping for breath) You know, I'm single and I was wondering if. . .

Atalanta: Meleager, you don't look well. You're sweating! (touching his forehead) You've got a terrible fever!

Meleager: I feel like I'm burning up! Please, get me some water. . .

Servant 1: (in the palace) Your highness, the fire is almost out!

Artemis: Atalanta raced to a nearby stream. She cupped her hands and caught up some water and returned to Meleager's side. When she returned, she found Meleager dead! In just a short time, she had fallen in love with him. Now he was gone.

Atalanta: Some god's hand is in this! Here's what I say to you: since you've taken away the man I loved, I'll never love another!

Artemis: With that, Atalanta disappeared into the forest, swearing in her heart that she would never, ever marry.

Scene Four: Risky Business

Artemis: Atalanta wanted to be left alone, but she was a little too late. News of the great boar hunt had spread far and wide, as had the word about her beauty. Her father, the king who had cruelly abandoned her at birth, came forward and invited her to live in his palace. There, young men eager to win her approval began camping out around the palace door.

Servant 2: Atalanta, what should I tell those men outside? They say they won't go home until you promise to marry one of them. Something's got to be done, because we can't get anything done around here with that crowd blocking the doorway.

Atalanta: Send them away. Tell them I hate every one of them!

Servant 2: We tried that already, remember? They don't listen to us. Please, you go talk to them!

Atalanta: All right, but it's not going to be pretty.

Artemis: Atalanta appeared at the gates of her father's castle and was swarmed by the hopeful suitors.

Suitor 1: Marry me and you'll never want to look at another man!

Suitor 2: If you marry me, I promise I'll stay right by your side forever!

Atalanta: If you all are trying to scare me, it's working. (frustrated) Okay, I'll marry one of you.

Suitors 1 and 2: Yes!

Atalanta: The one who beats me in a race, that is.

Suitor 1: We can't do that! You're as fast as lightning.

Suitor 2: Hey, there's no harm in trying, is there? I'll give it a shot! You might slip or something.

Atalanta: Oh, I forgot to mention the catch. If you win, you get to marry me. But if I win, it's death for the loser, and I'm serious!

Suitor 1: Well, Atalanta, maybe you're right. We can just be friends.

Suitor 2: I. . .I just remembered that I've got a problem with my Achilles heel. Better not race today. . .See you later!

Artemis: Surprisingly enough, not all the suitors gave up. Some were so in love with Atalanta that they did race her, even though it cost them their lives.

Atalanta: (speaking to a loser) Sorry about this, but I tried to warn you.

Artemis: One day a young man named Hippomenes came by to see a determined suitor challenge Atalanta. He couldn't believe that anyone would risk his life for some woman's hand in marriage. Then he saw Atalanta.

Hippomenes: (lovestruck) I must marry that woman or I'll die! The only problem is, I'll most likely die trying to marry her. Hmm. . .I think I'll need some divine help with this one.

Artemis: Hippomenes asked for help from Aphrodite, the goddess of love. Aphrodite—who was none too pleased that Atalanta had sworn she would never love again—gave him three

beautiful golden apples and a plan to win Atalanta's hand. The next day Hippomenes appeared at Atalanta's door.

Atalanta: Not another one! Don't you know what will happen to you?

Hippomenes: But I'm sure I'll win this race. I feel that the gods are on my side.

Atalanta: Some people just can't take a hint. Please. Do yourself a favor and fall in love with someone else.

Artemis: But the next morning Atalanta found herself on the starting line with the confident young man. Hippomenes knew he stood in the very spot where so many unfortunate suitors had stood before him. The signal was given and the race began. For the first hundred yards, Hippomenes managed to keep up with Atalanta. But then she started to take off.

Hippomenes: I'd better put my plan into action!

Artemis: The young man took out one of the golden apples he'd hidden in his tunic. He tossed a dazzling apple in Atalanta's path.

Atalanta: I'll just stop to pick it up. After all, I've got him beat already.

Artemis: When Atalanta stopped, Hippomenes managed to get the lead. But when Atalanta got back in the race, she quickly made up for lost time.

Hippomenes: (puffing) Time for me to use my second apple. . .Just. . .throw. . .this one. . .to the right.

Artemis: Atalanta went after this apple too, although it took her way off course. She looked up and saw her opponent far ahead of her.

Atalanta: I've got to stop playing. This race is getting serious!

Artemis: Coming into the homestretch, the runners were neck and neck. Hippomenes knew that he had no chance against Atalanta unless he used his brain.

Hippomenes: (wheezing) My last apple. . .Hope. . .it. . .works. . .

Artemis: He tossed his last shining, shimmering globe right in Atalanta's path. Though she knew stopping would cost her the race, she couldn't help herself. That third apple looked even more inviting than the other two. When Atalanta looked up from the apple, she saw Hippomenes crossing the finish line.

Hippomenes: (collapsing) Atalanta. . .I've won. . .Now. . .marry me?

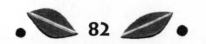

Atalanta: (barely winded) Yes, I'll keep my word—even if using those apples wasn't exactly fair—and be your bride.

Artemis: And so they were married. There is another story about Atalanta and Hippomenes that says they were turned into lions by Aphrodite—who was angry that Hippomenes never came back to thank her for her help—but that tale will have to wait for another day. . .

The End

FOR THE TEACHER

Talk About It

- Why did Atalanta's father abandon her when she was a baby? Why did he invite her back into his life later on? Is it surprising that Atalanta goes back to live with him? Why or why not?

- What makes Atalanta stand out from other Greek heroes? What kind of person is she? Use examples from the play to back up your descriptions.

- In this myth, the future is shown to be controlled by a group of old knitters named the Fates. How does Queen Althaea outwit their prediction about her son's life? Is she successful in the long run? Why or why not?

Extension Activities

- **Looking Back** Help students imagine that they are Atalanta as an old woman, looking back on life. What kind of autobiography would she write? Would she have any regrets? How did she feel at certain key times and about certain key people? Would she have lived life any differently? Challenge them to put their imaginary autobiographies on paper.

- **Unfair!** Throughout this story Atalanta faces discrimination because of her gender. Ask your students to remember times, both past and present, when people have faced prejudice. Make a list on the blackboard of areas in which discrimination can occur (race, religion, etc.), examples of progress fighting these injustice and examples of setbacks.

- **Legacy** Atalanta is one of the first in a long line of celebrated female athletes. Challenge students to make posters celebrating other female heroes of sport. Encourage students to research athletes from the past as well as the present, and local heroes as well as national or world heroes. If a local hero such as a high-school or college student is available, invite her to come share with the class what it took for her to become a top-notch competitor in her field. Have students be prepared to tell her a short version of the Atalanta myth in case she's never heard it.

PUTTING IT TOGETHER

Talk About It

- What would it have been like to be a girl growing up in ancient Greece? A boy? What would you have spent most of your time doing? What would you have liked best about your life?

- How would you describe the gods and goddesses of Greece, based on their behavior in these myths? Would humans have been better off if the gods didn't mess around so much in people's lives? Why or why not?

- Greek myths didn't have happy endings very often, as is clear from these plays. Their humans and gods were also very moody, doing good one second and evil the next. How does this differ from many of the stories we read, hear and watch today?

- Do you think ancient Greeks would agree or disagree with the statement, "life is fair"? Why? How does this differ from our own attitudes about life and what it owes us?

Extension Activities

- **Myths, American Style** After completing the discussion above and the "Legacy" activity below, encourage small groups of students to brainstorm a new version of one of this book's myths, setting it in the United States, with an "American" sensibility. Some may wish to make theirs funny, with improbable (to Greeks) "happy endings," while others may wish to keep more closely to the original form. What kinds of changes alter the stories the least? The most?

- **Family Tree** Encourage students to make an illustrated family tree in which they list the major gods and goddesses of Greek mythology, and their relationships to each other. (Remind students that the Greeks and Romans gave different names to similar gods.)

- **Legacy** Encourage students to find examples of how Greek names they've encountered in myths continue to resonate today. Examples can be found in place names (Aegean Sea; Troy AL, IL, KS, MI, MO, NY, NC, OH, PA; Sparta GA, IL, MI, NJ, NC, TN, WI), product and team names (Honda Odyssey, Helen of Troy hair-care products, USC Trojans), and so forth. Challenge groups to contribute their findings to a classroom mural.

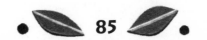

ADDITIONAL READING

Some Primary Works (available in a variety of editions and translations)

Homer, *The Iliad*

Homer, *The Odyssey*

Ovid, *Metamorphoses*

Virgil, *The Aeneid*

Some Reference Books and Retellings

Bullfinch, Thomas. *The Age of Fable* (Doubleday)

Church, Alfred. *The Aeneid for Boys and Girls* (Macmillan)

Evslin, Bernard. *Greeks Bearing Gifts* (Scholastic)

Grant, Michael. *Myths of the Greeks and Romans* (New American Library)

Graves, Robert. *Greek Gods and Heroes* (Dell)

Graves, Robert. *The Greek Myths* (Penguin)

Hamilton, Edith. *Mythology* (New American Library)

Rouse, W.H.D. *Gods, Heroes and Men of Ancient Greece* (New American Library)

NOTES

NOTES